# CUTTING TIES WITH DARKNESS

## 2 CORINTHIANS

T0324281

**Other titles in
the Transformative Word series:**

*God Behind the Scenes: The Book of Esther*
by Wayne Barkhuizen

*When You Want to Yell at God: The Book of Job*
by Craig G. Bartholomew

*Revealing the Heart of Prayer: The Gospel of Luke*
By Craig G. Bartholomew

*Between the Cross and the Throne: The Book of Revelation*
by Matthew Emerson

# CUTTING TIES WITH DARKNESS

## 2 CORINTHIANS

### TRANSFORMATIVE WORD

JOHN D. BARRY

Edited by Craig G. Bartholomew

LEXHAM PRESS

Print ISBN 9781577996064
Digital ISBN 9781577996071

Series Editor: Craig G. Bartholomew
Academic Editor: Derek R. Brown
Research Assistant: Abby Salinger
Developmental Editor: David Bomar
Assistant Editors: Rebecca Brant, Lynnea Fraser,
    Abigail Stocker, Joel Wilcox
Cover Design: Patrick Fore
Back Cover Design: Brittany Schrock
Typesetting: ProjectLuz.com

To my dear friend Paul Foth,
who calls me to center my life on Jesus.

And to all who seek freedom in Jesus' name—
you will find it.

# TABLE OF CONTENTS

# INTRODUCTION: THE THREADS OF LIFE

"How do you pick up the threads of an old life? How do you go on, when in your heart, you begin to understand, there is no going back? There are some things that time cannot mend. Some hurts that go too deep." When Frodo Baggins says these words at the end of the movie *The Return of the King*, they carry the full weight of someone who is grieving deeply.[1] These words echo some of my relationships. I often wonder: "With all the damage that has been done, how can we ever return to how things used to be?" And, "Was there ever really anything to our friendship at all?" This is how Paul must have felt when he wrote 2 Corinthians. In this deeply personal letter, Paul offers profound insights into relationships. He writes out of both love and pain. He writes about severing relationships and mending them. He writes in a way that is decidedly centered on God, as seen in the person of Christ. Paul is humble and meek; he is bold and adamant.[2] But I don't want to give away the punchline here; I'll let Paul do that as we journey together through past hurts and intelligent solutions—as we learn what darkness is and how to cut ties with it.

## Overview

Second Corinthians is a letter laced with pain. Paul has suffered greatly for the good news of Jesus, and now he is struggling to maintain a relationship with the church he founded in Corinth (1 Cor 3:6; 2 Cor 1:8–2:4). Paul planted the church at Corinth while there as a tentmaker for at least a year and a half (Acts 18:1–18).[3] By Christ's strength, Paul built the church at Corinth from nothing into a lively church, proclaiming the gospel of God to them "without payment" (2 Cor 11:7–9).

---

**SETTING**

The events described in 2 Corinthians likely occurred during Paul's third missionary journey (ca. AD 52–57). Paul founded the church at Corinth during his second missionary journey (Acts 18; ca. AD 49–51).

---

But sometime after departing Corinth, Paul learned that the Corinthian church was allowing Christians to openly practice sexual immorality (1 Cor 5:9–11). To put a stop to this, Paul wrote a letter demanding that the believers not associate with people who claim to believe in Jesus but openly live in sin (1 Cor 5:9). There is no preserved copy of this initial letter to Corinth; all we can know about it we learn from 1 Corinthians (which actually is his second letter to Corinth).

After sending his initial letter, Paul received a report from a church member that factions were emerging in the church (1 Cor 1:1). Around the same time as this report, the Corinthians apparently sent him a letter full of pragmatic questions.[4] To address these issues, Paul wrote his second letter to them—1 Corinthians.

In 1 Corinthians, Paul explains that he does not want the Corinthian church to separate from all people who live in sin because that would mean separating from the world entirely; instead, they should separate from those who claim to believe in Jesus but condone sin (1 Cor 5:10–11).[5] Paul considers this issue to be so detrimental to the church that he tells the Corinthians to "remove the evil person from among yourselves" (1 Cor 5:13; compare 2 Cor 6:14–7:1).[6]

Sometime after he sent 1 Corinthians, Paul had a "sorrowful visit" to Corinth, during which people had argued with Paul about the changes he felt they should make (2 Cor 13:2). This resulted in Paul writing a "sorrowful letter" to the Corinthians—another letter that has not been preserved for us today (see 2 Cor 2:3–4; 7:8, 12). Following this letter, Paul wrote a fourth letter,[7] which we know as 2 Corinthians.

In 2 Corinthians, we see that Paul's correspondence with the Corinthians has done little to change their ways. They have repented by dismissing at least one problematic believer and now have found a way toward reconciliation with that person, but not much else has changed (2 Cor 2:5–11). Tragically, at least some members of the Corinthian church still have problems with Paul and his authority and are now following false apostles (2 Cor 11:1–15). They also seem to be openly living in sin and welcoming other so-called believers who are living in sin (2 Cor 12:20–21). But the stakes are even higher than just the well-being of the Corinthian church: The lives of impoverished people in Jerusalem hang in the balance as they wait for an offering from the Corinthian believers (2 Cor 9:1–3). The work of the gospel reaching the ends of the earth is also in view, since Paul intends to use the church at Corinth as a launching point for bringing the good news of Jesus to unreached regions (2 Cor 10:16). If the Corinthians don't cut ties with darkness, only pain will come to them and others. Jesus has a better way, if only they can see it and embrace it.

This context explains all of 2 Corinthians. When Paul says, "Do not be unequally yoked," he means first, that we should not associate with believers who don't actually live for Jesus, and second, that engaging in any sort of intimate relationship or partnership with someone who does not let Jesus be the center of their lives will ultimately lead to our demise (2 Cor 6:14). We must cut ties with whatever or whomever leads us to darkness.

Paul intends for believers to engage with people who don't share their beliefs; he just doesn't want to see their relationships lead them into darkness. The Corinthians believers are supposed to be changing the world, not to be changed by it. Paul wants to see the Corinthian believers separate from their old way of living and fully embrace the ways of Jesus.

In 2 Corinthians we see that Paul feels responsible for the Corinthians, both as an apostle and as a brother in Christ (2 Cor 1:1; 11:2).[8] Paul cannot simply let the Corinthian believers go their own way; he reaches out to resolve the conflicts that have arisen, and he hopes the Corinthians will work with him. Paul might be unable to pick up his old life with the Corinthians, but he still wants to move forward with them. He has ideas about what it means to live under Jesus' new covenant—ideas that he believes will change the Corinthians' lives and ultimately bring them back into relationship with him.

But this is complicated: There are false leaders, and old friends turned enemies, and broken relationships. There are questions about Paul's motives and ministry. He is essentially standing on trial before a body of believers that he planted himself, and he knows that *they* are the ones unable to stand the test of authenticity (2 Cor 10:7–8; 12:19–21; 13:5–8). And nothing with the Corinthians is clear; it's opaque and in the shadows. Paul has to wade through the gray areas of life to find answers. And isn't that exactly how life is for all of us?

A heretic never says, "I'm a heretic." A deceiver never alerts you to his true intentions, and a friend can turn on you at any moment. A family member, or even a spouse, can betray your trust. Authenticity and reliability are hard to find, and so are real friends. Giving each other the benefit of the doubt is far from the norm. And correctly asserting truth, without standing in judgment of someone else, is decidedly difficult.

Some of the Corinthian believers seem to be struggling within themselves. They can't rightly see the difference between darkness and light because they have allowed darkness to take hold. Paul has so much to teach them, but most of them are blind to it.[9]

Paul's response teaches us much about how to work through troubled relationships. He shows us that we cannot truly know another person without first knowing ourselves. And we cannot overcome our demons without first separating ourselves from the work of Satan. In order to be set free, we have to cut ties with the darkness—and Paul tells us how.

For Paul, all of these difficulties are clarified when we renew our perspective in Christ: We were made to be empowered by God's Spirit so that everything we do is influenced by his holiness and love. As hard as it may be to admit, we are either acting for Jesus or against him; we are either centered on Christ or camping out with evil (2 Cor 5:1–10; 6:15). For some people, this is an intentional choice, or a choice made by default when they don't make a decision at all; for others, the choice comes by way of deception. Those yet to know Jesus are called to make a decision for him. Those who already know Jesus are called to choose him each day instead of choosing the influences of culture. Even those of us who know Jesus, like the Corinthian believers, risk being so influenced by evil that we can end up doing Satan's work without realizing it. This is why it's so critical that we center ourselves fully on Christ (2 Cor 1:1).

> In order to be set free, we have to cut ties with the darkness—and Paul tells us how.

To combat the darkness, Paul ultimately shows us a better way: We are not meant to pick up the threads of our old sinful lives at all; instead, we're called to rebuild our lives on the redemption we find in Jesus.[10]

## OUTLINE OF 2 CORINTHIANS

1. Introduction and blessing (2 Cor 1:1–11)

2. Paul's defense of his ministry and call to discernment (2 Cor 1:12–6:13)

3. The tough decisions Christians must make (2 Cor 6:14–7:1)

4. Peace and generosity toward Paul and others (2 Cor 7:2–9:15)

5. Paul's visit to Corinth, super-apostles, and the gospel (2 Cor 10:1–13:13)[11]

# The Center of 2 Corinthians

The strength of Paul's words could prompt us to say that, for him, the world is black and white. But when you get down to the gritty details of 2 Corinthians, it's apparent that the world is much more complicated than many of the "religious" people would like to believe. There isn't just "us" and "them." This isn't one political party versus another we're dealing with—or, as Americans say, "donkeys versus elephants." There are hyenas and lions, zebras and gazelles. The spectrum of Paul's worldview is as bright and colorful as a street market in India or downtown New York City. The whole world—everyone, everything—is made by one Creator. There is potential for everything to once again be good and do good—for all things to be saved by Jesus and to be empowered to live in God's image (2 Cor 3:17–18; compare Gen 1:27; Rom 8:19–23). With this in mind, Paul says, "Do not be unequally yoked with unbelievers. For what partnership is there between righteousness and lawlessness? Or what fellowship has light with darkness? And what agreement does Christ have with Beliar? What does a believer share with an unbeliever?" (2 Cor 6:14–15).[12] Paul is not contrasting black and white. Instead, Paul is interpreting how the universe functions now that Jesus has come. "Light" here does not mean "white"; it is the full spectrum of the light that first entered the universe—the spectrum we see in the rainbow, which is itself a promise from God (Gen 1:3–5; 9:12–17).[13] Paul is saying, "Look, there's darkness here. There is evil. God wants color and life, as we see in Christ. Which realm will you live in? Will you embrace Jesus' realm of life and light or stay in the darkness of all that defies its Creator?"

Paul shows us in 2 Corinthians that evil is not to be toyed with. Darkness only brings darkness. Light, on the other hand, overwhelms everything with its beauty, with its spectrum of color. It makes everything brighter and more wonderful. Light has hope, even in the most desperate circumstances—like tattered relationships.

> Darkness only brings darkness. Light, on the other hand, overwhelms everything with its beauty, with its spectrum of color.

Paul is not calling for Christians to follow a set of regulations to ensure purity; this is not what he means by light and darkness (compare Gal 2:16; 3:11–12).[14] Instead, Paul is talking about living in God's ways or choosing another path; he is talking about what is healthy and peaceful versus what only causes destruction. God's ways are good; everything else will lead you astray and ultimately just hurt you. In addition, the other path—the one that goes against God's ways—can be chosen by default. Not choosing is choosing, so we must be aware of our choices and their consequences. By ignoring the effects of their day-to-day decisions, and the fact that many of their decisions are motivated by their culture's values, some of the Corinthian believers have been led astray. They have allowed corrupt ideas to enter into their lives, and consequently they have followed the peddlers of those ideas. Instead, they should have turned to the one who originally led them to Jesus—Paul—to show them the way forward.

Unlike Frodo's story at the end of *The Return of the King*, the story of the Corinthians was not yet written. And that meant there was a chance for them to turn a corner—to offer a better narrative with their lives.[15] The Corinthians could choose to see the full spectrum of light and bask in it, or they could remain in the darkness. Their relationships needed mending, and evil needed to be purged from their lives, but there was still time and hope.

Paul aims to show the Corinthians that they must continually center themselves in the full spectrum of God's light—and live in wonderment of him. They need to see and believe how Christ changes absolutely everything. They need to understand how Jesus can restore health to their relationships and give them an intelligent approach to every decision they face. They need to see that Jesus has sufficient grace, even when they struggle (2 Cor 12:9).

**SUGGESTED READING**

- ☐ 2 Corinthians 1:3–4
- ☐ 2 Corinthians 6:14–7:1
- ☐ 2 Corinthians 12:9

## Reflection

What parts of your story are left to be written? What has God revealed to you that has not yet come to pass?

_____

_____

_____

What relationships do you have that are strained and require discernment? List them and pray about them.

_____

_____

_____

Honesty time: Reflect upon the threads of darkness running through your life and ask God for wisdom about overcoming them. What are those threads?

_____

_____

_____

# THE TOUGH DECISIONS CHRISTIANS MUST MAKE

## 2 Corinthians 6:14–7:1

We're going start this journey with 2 Corinthians in the middle of the letter—because all of the concerns Paul has with the Corinthian church really come back to the ideas he brings up in 2 Corinthians 6:14–7:1. If you're unequally yoked with unbelievers, you will be led astray. And if you're led astray, you will naturally turn on those who truly live for Jesus. If Paul is to defend his apostleship and rebuild his relationship with the Corinthian church, then he must first get them on track with Jesus—and that means showing them how to cut ties with darkness. That means teaching them that his relationship with them is built on the principles of the new covenant of Jesus, not on the viewpoints of their culture or local leaders. In 2 Corinthians 6:14–7:1 Paul says:

> Do not be unequally yoked with unbelievers. For what partnership [is there] between righteousness and lawlessness? Or what fellowship [has] light with darkness? And what agreement does Christ [have] with Beliar? What does a believer share with an unbeliever? And what agreement [has the] temple of God with idols? For we are a temple of [the] living God.[1] Just as God said, "I will dwell in them and walk among [them], and I will be their God and they will be my people." Therefore "come out from [the] middle of them and be separate," says [the] Lord, "and do not touch an unclean thing and I will receive you. And I will be to you a father, and you will be to me sons and daughters," says [the] Lord Almighty. Since we have these promises, beloved, let us cleanse ourselves from every defilement of flesh and spirit[2] bringing to completion holiness in [the] fear of God.[3]

> If you're unequally yoked with unbelievers, you will be led astray. And if you're led astray, you will naturally turn on those who truly live for Jesus.

It's not a comfortable subject for our generation, but the concept of "defilement" thematically underlies the entire passage of 2 Corinthians 6:14–7:1—and, in a sense, all of 2 Corinthians. The passage begins with the command: "Do not be unequally yoked with unbelievers" (2 Cor 6:14). At this point we naturally ask: "Why not?" The answer to this question is offered in 2 Corinthians 7:1, where Paul says: "Let us cleanse ourselves from every defilement."[4] The "unbelievers" bring "defilement" to believers. In other words, Paul is saying, "Do not be unequally yoked with unbelievers because they will defile you—cleanse yourself of them." At first, Paul's words may sound harsh and wrong, but when we get into the details of his argument, they make sense. As he explains in 7:1, "holiness" is brought "to completion" in the church by the "cleansing" of the community from "every defilement," as well as by the "cleansing" of each individual.[5]

> **TERM TO KNOW**
>
> A *hapax legomenon* refers to a word that appears only once in a given text or group of texts, making it difficult to accurately define. Second Corinthians 7:1 is the only place in the entire New Testament where the word *molysmou* appears. Through researching the word's semantic domain and usage outside of the New Testament, we can conclude the word likely means "defilement" in this context.

When Paul talks about defilement, he has in view how dangerous it is for a Christian to be influenced by someone who has not accepted Jesus as Lord. Paul does not say that Christians should stop talking with unbelievers; he says that the worldviews of a Christian and an unbeliever are fundamentally opposed, so they should not partner together. Since the unbelievers at Corinth have a keen association with idols, there is no doubt in Paul's mind that their influence can defile the believers, both in "flesh" (outwardly) and "spirit" (inwardly). This does not necessarily mean that the unbelievers literally are "defilement," but rather that they can be a source of defile-

> A worldview centered on Jesus doesn't just result in beliefs; it results in actions.

ment for Christians who become too heavily involved with them. For this reason, believers who have already been negatively influenced by unbelievers must now cleanse themselves from "all defilement of flesh and spirit."[6]

It should be the goal of the Christian to influence non-Christians, to bring them to Jesus—not to simply be a friend that appeases them, for that will only lead to the Christian living according to the unbeliever's worldview. The believer is called to bring the unbeliever to belief, repentance, and purity, not to give in to the unbeliever's ways and become defiled. The particular unbelievers that Paul has in view are preventing the believers from centering their lives on Christ. The unbelievers are getting in the way of generosity and causing the believers to neglect their calling as ambassadors of Christ's reconciliation (e.g., 2 Cor 4:1–6; 5:16–20; 8:1–14; 9).

When we center our lives on Jesus, we naturally carry out his reconciliatory work (2 Cor 5:16–21). As such, believers must sever themselves from the influence of Satan (2 Cor 6:15).[7] A worldview centered on Jesus doesn't just result in beliefs; it results in actions. Thus, the Corinthian problem is really a theological problem.

## Not Just Belief, but Action

Second Corinthians 6:14–7:1 emerges from the context of Paul's defense of his apostleship in 2:14–7:4. Paul shows that there are overarching theological matters at work in the Corinthian community that need to be addressed if the church is to understand his apostleship and respect him once more (e.g., 2 Cor 2:14–17; 5:1–10). Their problems with Paul are rooted in their problems with living for Jesus.

Without centering themselves on the work of Christ and separating from evil, the Corinthian believers won't understand the larger missionary scope of Paul's endeavors (e.g., 2 Cor 9; 10:1–6; 11:1–14). For example, if the Corinthian believers were living in God's ways, they would be able to see for themselves that Paul's plans were always subject to God's intervention, and Paul likely wouldn't need to explain himself (2 Cor 1:12–2:13). Once the Corinthian believers cut ties with darkness, they will understand Paul and be able to renew their relationship with him.

In light of this, 2 Corinthians 6:14–7:1 is really about the divisions that unbelievers have caused to occur between Paul and the Corinthian community. The passage highlights a major point of the letter: The effectiveness of the Corinthian community is dependent upon whether they will choose to separate themselves from unbelievers. Their "separation" will result in an affirmation of Paul, the gospel, and, most of all, Christ; their choice to not "separate" will result in a denial. Paul realizes this, and to make the point he "rhetorically digresses" in 2 Corinthians 6:14–7:1 to explain the full effect of the choice before the Corinthian believers.[8]

The proper path forward for our lives is living "in the fear of God" (2 Cor 7:1).[9] Truly loving God means fearing him—realizing that he is capable of great and mighty deeds and living in awe of that. The "fear of God" is what *causes* believers to separate themselves from unbelievers. It's what leads us to call those in our church to live according to God's purposes (2 Cor 5:12–13). It's what leads us to make the tough day-to-day decisions to stay on track with Christ.

When Paul uses the Greek term *aphorizō* (ἀφορίζω), translated as "to separate," he is suggesting that believers be active in setting themselves apart for the gospel's work.[10] This is not about removing ourselves from all those who don't believe in Jesus; Paul directly disagrees with that interpretation (1 Cor 5:9–10). Instead, Paul is telling us to make a concerted effort to ensure that we are set apart for Christ's work and that we don't allow anything or anyone to impede that. Since Paul knows that the easiest way for Christ's work to be impeded is by partnering too closely with unbelievers—thus allowing for their influence to be more powerful than Jesus' in our lives—he commands us to separate from "the middle of them"—their territory, where they have too much control over us. Practically, this means that we cannot allow for unbelievers to influence the direction of our families, churches, businesses, and lives. We cannot live in their midst; instead, we must bring them into the midst of Christ. We don't cater to them; we show them Jesus.

# The Frightening Reality of Being Unequally Yoked

Each decision we make affects our relationship with Jesus—either positively or negatively. This is perhaps most true when it comes to the people we surround ourselves with—the people we allow to influence us.

Paul commands the Corinthian believers to "not be unequally yoked with unbelievers" (2 Cor 6:14). The Greek term behind the translation "unequally yoked" (*heterozygountes*, ἑτεροζυγοῦντες) occurs only this one time in the New Testament, but it also occurs—although in a slightly different form—in the Septuagint (ancient Greek translation) of Leviticus 19:19, which prohibits mating two different kinds of animals. The term also reflects the tradition of Deuteronomy 22:10, where there is a prohibition against plowing with a donkey and ox. Both texts contain the tradition that two different kinds of animals, working together to either reproduce or plow a field, is wrong. Paul appropriates this idea to emphasize that the partnering of believers with unbelievers is an unhealthy situation.[11]

But this leaves us with a question: How do we define an unbeliever? Paul leaves his language ambiguous, allowing us to apply his "severance" language to all the conflicts facing the Corinthian believers. Based on the content of 2 Corinthians and the historical context of the letter, there are three possible ways to define the unbelievers: idolaters; conflict-ridden and anti-Paul detractors; or simply anyone who doesn't believe in Jesus.[12]

Broadly speaking, an unbeliever (*apistos*, ἄπιστος) is anyone who has not chosen to believe in Jesus as the Lord of their life. In 1 Corinthians 6:3 Paul uses the term to refer to those who go to public court before their unbelieving peers. But unbelievers don't exist just outside church gatherings; they're welcome in church gatherings too (1 Cor 14:22–24)—which is yet another testament that Paul is not telling us to completely separate ourselves from unbelievers in 2 Corinthians 6:14–7:1, but instead to avoid particular kinds of relationships.[13]

In 1 Corinthians 7:12–15 *apistos* is used more narrowly to refer to those who have spouses who don't believe in Jesus—a usage that directly parallels 2 Corinthians 6:14. Here, Paul is clear that someone already married who comes to Christ, and has a spouse who has not accepted Christ, should stay married to the unbelieving spouse.[14]

In the context of 2 Corinthians and the Corinthian community in general, the first kind of unbelievers who bring "defilement" are idolaters (1 Cor 8:7; 2 Cor 6:16). Historically, idolaters would have been everywhere in Corinth, since, as archaeology has revealed, there were countless altars, temples, and tributes to Greek gods and the Roman imperial cults in Corinth around AD 50–100.[15] Paul's viewpoint in 2 Corinthians 6:14 is further clarified in 1 Corinthians 10, where he tells believers to go to unbelievers' houses to eat when they're invited, but if they learn that the food has been sacrificed to idols, to refrain from eating—for their own sake and for the sake of the unbeliever (1 Cor 10:23–30).

Paul first confirms the idolatry problem among the Corinthian church in 1 Corinthians 8:7, where he states, "But some, being accustomed until now to the

idol, eat ... food ... sacrificed to idols, and their conscience, because it is weak, is defiled." This particular usage is of special significance since Paul uses a
verb for "defilement" related to the noun "defilement"
used in 2 Corinthians 7:1. Thus the "defilement" of
the unbelievers is likely caused by their idolatrous,
or at least idol-affiliated, practices (whether they be
conscious or unconscious). Their unbelief in God is
directly linked to their belief in idols. The phrase,
"What agreement [has the] temple of God with idols?"
in 2 Corinthians 6:15 also elucidates the argument
that idolatry is one of the primary "defilements" of
the unbelievers.

Paul's language directly derives from his use of
temple imagery: "And what agreement [has the] temple of God with idols? For we are a temple of [the] living God" (2 Cor 6:16). Paul also says in 1 Corinthians:
"Do you not know that you are God's temple and the
Spirit of God dwells in you?" (1 Cor 3:16). The Jerusalem
temple—which would have been Paul's framework
for a holy temple where God's presence dwelled,
and likewise the framework for the Jewish people at
Corinth—was a holy place. There were rituals upon
rituals, primarily in the forms of sacrifices, to ensure
that people were holy enough (set apart enough) to
enter. When Paul looks at the Corinthian church and
sees that they are allowing unbelievers to draw them
away from Christ, he is shocked. How could people
who live as God's very presence on earth—his holy
temple—live this way? Paul is essentially saying,
"This isn't set-apart living; something must change."

The Holy Spirit should have been transforming the
believers at Corinth, but instead they were allowing

themselves to be transformed by falsehoods. They should have been imaging God on earth, but instead they were imaging the values of their culture.

Idolatry has a powerful hold on many people, both in Paul's time and our own. Today, idols often come in the form of television, online media (such as social networks), or even people in our lives. Paul shows us that when we follow unbelievers, who don't have the ability to distinguish between idolatry and God's ways, we can easily fall victim to their vices.

Idolatry was a primary issue for the Corinthian church (1 Cor 8; 10). It was such a problem that Paul offered extensive warnings about food offered to idols—making it clear that if the eating of food offered to idols by one person causes another person to worship idols (consciously or unconsciously), then the first person should stop eating food offered to idols (1 Cor 8:12–13). It's very possible that Paul's warning in 1 Corinthians 8:12–13 was ignored, resulting in his command for the believers to avoid close relationships with unbelieving idolaters (2 Cor 6:14, 17; 7:1). It may be that Paul no longer feels that the Corinthian community can choose their own plan of action on a situational basis, but instead needs an overall command. Paul explains the danger of having close partnerships with unbelievers earlier in his letter when he says, "The god of this age has blinded the minds of the unbelievers, so that they would not see the light of the gospel of the glory of Christ, who

> The Corinthians should have been imaging God on earth, but instead they were imaging the values of their culture.

is the image of God" (2 Cor 4:4). If the unbeliever is blinded by the god of this age, then they will see everything according to a different viewpoint.

Some of the unbelievers may very well be Paul's opponents, the "super-apostles" (2 Cor 11:5). Since the "super-apostles" are actually false apostles who have "led astray" the Corinthian community "from a pure devotion to Christ," they too could be associated with unbelievers in the "truth of Christ" (2 Cor 11:3, 10, 13).[16] Paul even associates the false apostles with the serpent and Satan (2 Cor 11:1-3, 14). For these adversaries, Paul sees little way forward, but this doesn't preclude any solution. It's possible that the same solution that was reached for the one who "caused pain" could be reached for the false apostles (2 Cor 2:5-11). Either way, it's clear that the concept of reconciliation transcends normal boundaries (2 Cor 2:11).

## The Reign of Jesus and the Fight against Beliar

To support his command that believers not be unequally yoked, Paul uses a series of rhetorical questions to emphasize that someone who believes in Christ does not share a common worldview with the unbeliever (2 Cor 6:14-15). As Paul explained earlier (2 Cor 4), the unbelievers have not seen the "light of the gospel of the glory of Christ, who is the image of God," because "the god of this world has blinded [their] minds" (2 Cor 4:4).[17] On the other hand, "the light of the knowledge of the glory of God in the face of Jesus Christ" has shined in the hearts of Paul and his fellow missionaries (2 Cor 4:6).[18] In other words, the unbelievers are looking for a god in the sphere of this world when they should be looking to Christ.

In one rhetorical question, Paul asks whether Christ has anything in common with Beliar (6:15). Beliar is an actual spiritual entity in the mind of Paul and represents "lawlessness," immorality, sexual sins, and deceit (e.g., *Testament of Asher* 1:8; 3:2; *Testament of Levi* 3:3; *Testament of Reuben* 4:11; 1QM 13:11). Beliar is probably another of Paul's terms for Satan, with whom Paul views believers as engaged in spiritual battle.[19] But this spiritual battle has very real implications for the Corinthians' relationships. The questioning structure of 2 Corinthians 6:14–16 challenges the heart and devotion of the entire Corinthian community. In 2 Corinthians 6:16 the temple of God and idols are contrasted rhetorically in order to emphasize the necessity for believers to avoid fellowship with idolaters, just as Christ has no accord with Beliar (2 Cor 6:15). The Corinthians must do this because they "are a temple of the living God" (2 Cor 6:16).[20]

Paul is urging the Corinthian believers to cut any close ties they have with unbelievers and to reconcile themselves with Christ and with one another (2 Cor 2:5–11; 5:11–16). Since "in Christ" there is "new creation," the Corinthian believers must live lives of generous reconciliation (2 Cor 5:17–18; 9:6–12).

> Jesus' realm is all that is good, lovely, and wonderful—it is the spectrum of light that we see in the rainbow. Beliar's realm is only darkness.

Paul is showing that Jesus' realm is all that is good, lovely, and wonderful—it is the spectrum of light that we see in the rainbow. Beliar's realm is only darkness. Jesus offers life in his light; he offers hope of a life lived in the beauty of God—a life that reflects God's image—while Beliar offers only death. Paul's point: Why let unbelievers draw you away from God and his purposes? It's better to separate from them than to be lost to their ways.

## Centering Our Lives on Christ

Since the Corinthian community is a "temple of [the] living God," they must find a way to maintain their status as a temple. This requires them to abide by, and understand, the authority of Paul, who is helping them live as people centered on Christ (2 Cor 6:16–18; 11:5–6; 12:11–12).[21] Paul has the authority to make this request because he is an "ambassador" and "apostle" (meaning a "sent one") "of Christ," "by the will of God" (2 Cor 1:1; 5:20).[22]

For Paul, a refusal to turn to God's ways is tantamount to choosing spiritual exile. Even a default decision of simply choosing to do nothing could result in this.[23] The believers are required to dissociate themselves from unbelievers not only in principle, but also in *action*—to move away from what is "unclean" (2 Cor 6:17). The "unclean thing[s]" are likely the "food offered to idols" mentioned in 1 Corinthians 8:7; they also could be the actions of unbelievers (i.e., the passage is emphasizing the connection between interpersonal associations and consequent actions). Thus, Paul may primarily have the avoidance of idolatry in mind (e.g., 2 Cor 6:16).

One of the sins that Paul is fighting against is the wrong kind of association with unbelievers—the kind that leads to a broken relationship with Christ. Instead of living like unbelievers, the believers are to center their lives on Jesus (e.g., 2 Cor 6:13; 7:2). In return, God will receive them (2 Cor 6:17; this idea emerges from Ezek 20:34). These ideas are all set against the tradition of God's covenant with his people. By evoking ideas involving God's covenants, Paul aims to show that it's best for believers to repent now, since God ultimately will require that of them anyway. This is part of what it means to live in the new covenant.[24]

## Finding Completion in Our God

It is only in God that we can find completion—wholeness. Anything less than our God will just leave us broken. People can't fill the God-sized hole in our hearts. Paul states that if we cleanse ourselves from defilement, then holiness will be brought to completion (2 Cor 7:1). We need our hearts to be cleansed by the living God—"the Son of God who bled and died and rose again for me."[25]

"Holiness will be brought to completion" by means of "the fear of God" (2 Cor 7:1). We are to live in "awe" of God and in obedience to him. The Corinthian community—and we, too, for that matter—must remain the temple of God (his indwelling) and, in doing so, work to bring the sphere of God to those who are still in the darkness (2 Cor 4:6). Some have been blinded and kept from "seeing the light" (2 Cor 4:4), but the believers cannot let these unbelievers prevent them from dwelling in the light.

In 2 Corinthians 6:14-7:1, Paul appears to digress only to reveal the focal point of the ethical discussion in his letter. In the midst of arguing for his apostleship, Paul has realized the larger issues that are at work in the Corinthian community. In return, he commands the believing Corinthian community to "be separate" from idolatrous, divisive, and anti-Pauline unbelievers, who are preventing them from centering themselves on Jesus, from being generous, and from living as reconciliatory ministers of the gospel of Christ. The defiling unbelievers are a hindrance to the holiness of the Corinthian community; therefore the believers must cleanse themselves "from every defilement of flesh and spirit" that has been brought upon them by separating themselves from these people. The Corinthian community—and all believers, for that matter—must believe in the one and only God who raised Lord Jesus, and who will raise them also with him (2 Cor 4:13-14). In doing this, they will be brought into God's presence and will see that his grace extends to all believers. We too, like the Corinthian community, must act on our beliefs by affirming the authority of the apostles, by bringing reconciliation to the world through faith in Jesus Christ, and by giving generously by the means of God, Christ, and the Spirit.

Christians have to make many difficult decisions, and many of them are based in our relationships. Which relationships should we maintain? Which are okay to let go of? And when should we cut ties with someone? Paul brings some clarity to all these questions in 2 Corinthians 6:14-7:1, which I view as the central argument of the letter.

Whenever we are being led astray from that goal, we must make changes, no matter how difficult those changes are.

**SUGGESTED READING**

- ☐  2 Corinthians 6:14–7:1
- ☐  1 Corinthians 7:12–24
- ☐  1 Corinthians 10:23–11:1

## Reflection

Do you think Paul's command to not be unequally yoked applies to marriage? Does it apply to business relationships?

_____

_____

_____

As we live in the spectrum of God's light, according to the colors of his creation, how should we handle darkness and those who represent it? How can we effectively minister to people without letting them lead us astray?

_____

_____

_____

# A GOD WHO COMFORTS US IN ALL AFFLICTION

## 2 Corinthians 1:3-11

> Blessed is the God and Father of our Lord Jesus Christ, the Father of mercies and God of all comfort, who comforts us in all our affliction, so that we may be able to comfort those who are in all affliction with the comfort with which we ourselves are comforted by God (2 Cor 1:3-4).

If only such poetry poured from our lips with each new day! Yet we easily think: "How can I praise God in the midst of this pain, sorrow, and struggle?" We also think upon our many sins against God and others—and the sins others have committed against us—until our entire outlook becomes laced with darkness. And it's all this darkness that stops us from praising the God who loves us. It is this worldview of darkness that Paul aims to disarm in 2 Corinthians. He wishes to mentally, emotionally, and spiritually place us where he himself is: fully centered on Jesus, who saves.

For Paul, praising God in the midst of affliction is not some lofty ideal. He knows suffering and grief all too well. He tells the Corinthians of the burden he experienced while spreading the gospel in the province of Asia (modern-day Turkey).[1] Paul says that he and Timothy were "burdened to an extraordinary degree, beyond our strength, so that we were in despair even of living" (2 Cor 1:8).

And in the middle of their despair, Paul and Timothy were far from alone—as the opening praise of 2 Corinthians tells us. God was with them.[2]

## PAUL AND TIMOTHY

Paul and Timothy wrote 2 Corinthians together, which is why Paul uses "we" throughout the letter. Paul and Timothy met in Lystra (Acts 16:1). Paul invited Timothy to join the second missionary journey likely because of his good standing and character (Acts 16:2). Paul mentored Timothy throughout his ministry, and he even calls Timothy his "brother" (2 Cor 1:1; Col 1:1; 1 Thess 3:2), his "son" (2 Cor 4:17; 1 Tim 1:2; 2 Tim 1:2), and his "fellow worker" (Rom 16:21; 1 Thess 3:2).

Paul shows us where he and Timothy find their resolve when he says: "But we ourselves had the sentence of death, in order that we would not put confidence in ourselves, but in the God who raises the dead" (2 Cor 1:9).[3] No matter what situation we might face, we can place our hope in the God who raises the dead. Resurrection hope is the *modus operandi* of

Christians. We operate on the basis of a God who saves and raises, a God who can do all things.

## Overcoming Depression with Joy

Like Paul, I know that I can have confidence in God because of my own experiences. With my own eyes, I have seen God work in the lives of others. And I know God to be true to his Word because of the very state of my heart. But to understand the state of my heart now versus the state of how it used to be, I need to tell you a story.

When I was 16, my longtime girlfriend, whom I thought I would marry someday, came over to my house and broke off our relationship. She told me that she "needed to find herself," and she couldn't do that if I was part of the equation. As I walked her to her car, it began to rain. I looked at the sky and said, "It always rains." The saying "when it rains, it pours" came to mind—which is humorous, in retrospect, since I live in the Pacific Northwest, where it always rains.

Now, before you write off this story as a silly high-school romance, give me a moment to explain. My girlfriend breaking up with me led to a downward spiral—a spiral that felt like Trent Reznor's lyrics: "I wear this crown of thorns upon my liar's chair / Full of broken thoughts I cannot repair / Beneath the stains of time, the feelings disappear / You are someone else, I am still right here."[4] In the words of this lyricist, whose music I can't even listen to any longer, I found my song of agony, my lament. I then wrote some of the darkest words of my life as I indulged my own demons of darkness. As I sank deeper into the spiral, I lost myself.[5] I idealized a woman who never existed, wondering why she had left me; and I idealized a person who I used to be—also a person who never existed. Depression deceived me, turning me against myself and nearly everyone else in my life. My own words lied to me as I read them back in the night.

Over a long period of counseling, I found that all this began long before the girlfriend. This wasn't really about her at all; it was about my own problems and the difficulties of childhood. Things were rough for me, to say the least. I was forced to grow up at age 10—in a matter of minutes as I watched my entire home life fall apart. And then I never confronted that reality again until seven years later, after the breakup. I had wrongly believed that my girlfriend could make my hurt go away, and now *she* was gone.

I began confronting my demons one by one, over a period of six months. I was casting them out—or at least aside—through prayer and Bible study. I was reading the book of Job and working through the cycles of grief.[6] At the same time, I was reading through the entire Bible.

> As Satan fought for my soul—using depression, anxiety, pain, and other things—God fought for it through his Word.

As I worked through each stage of my past, I began to give it to God—to place my burdens on the strong shoulders of Jesus. The Bible helped me to understand my past pain, to confront my present grief, and to find a new future without my girlfriend.[7] In the pages of Scripture, I found something truly transformative. I had always loved the Bible, but now it was riveting and moving. As Satan fought for my soul—using depression, anxiety, pain, and other things—God fought for it through his Word.

I got well through Jesus. Near the end of my depression, I decided I needed a major change in my life, so I applied for a study-abroad program in London. Even though I was way past the deadline, somehow I got in; and even though I didn't have a current passport, somehow I managed to get one in two weeks. When my feet hit the ground in London, I knew that I had made it. I was on the other side, and something awoke in my soul. The song to represent this time didn't come to me until later (it probably wasn't even written yet), but here's how it goes: "How fickle my heart and how woozy my eyes / I struggle to find any truth in your lies / And now my heart stumbles on things I don't know / My weakness I feel I must finally show ... Awake my soul, awake my soul."[8]

Through the work of Christ, God wrote a new song through my life. It's not like everything worked out once I arrived in London, or that I didn't struggle anymore with depression (because I did). But each time I leaned upon Jesus, my soul was totally free—and that awareness has never left me.

## To Live in Awe of the God Who Saves

The process of God working in us is the process of learning what it means to be truly human. It is not that we oppose the idea of being earthy creatures—who feel pain and mourn—but instead that we learn to understand our journey from God's

> The process of God working in us is the process of learning what it means to be truly human.

perspective. During my time of depression, Psalm 25—a psalm of deep sorrow and pain—was of great comfort to me. This psalm, along with many others, shows that the Bible confronts hardship and suffering realistically. But in doing so, it calls us into conversation with the living God, who can raise us from the dead (2 Cor 1:9). God cares about our anguish and feels pain with us (compare Isa 53; Psa 22). In the process of working through pain—and cutting ties with the darkness that unnecessarily holds us down—we find what it means to live as people who bear God's image.

As someone who is trying to live in God's image, the focus for Paul is not the trials he is enduring, but rather the God who is triumphant over them—a God most clearly seen in the personhood of Jesus. It is Jesus who "delivered" Paul and Timothy from the risk of "death," while they were in Asia, and it is Jesus who will "deliver" them again from whatever else might come their way (2 Cor 1:10). This is why they place their "hope" in Jesus—because Jesus is powerful enough to truly save.

For Paul, putting hope and confidence in Jesus means taking action—demonstrating faithful obedience to God and his promises even in the face of hardship. As God moves, so does Paul. Yet why is it so hard for us to move with God? Could it be that deep down, underneath it all, we don't really believe in the God we claim to believe in? If our God really is as strong as we say he is, why are we so afraid to address our pain to him?

Paul knew a God who could do anything. He believed in a God who could act on his behalf and a God who wanted to act on behalf of a community. Paul saw hope when others saw none. I know the same God that Paul knew. I know a God who can lift me up out of the pit, out of the miry clay (Psa 40). I know a God who can help me to sing a new song, one of praise and wonder. I know a God who can end the despair—who can bring healing to the most depressed heart.

So much of our pain comes from broken relationships. Some of these relationships are ones that we have wrongly put on a pedestal. We have held them up and esteemed them; we have given them a place that only God deserves. And in doing so we have made them a type of idol; we have replaced a crevice of our heart, sometimes even our whole hearts, with people rather than God (compare Matt 22:37). In 2 Corinthians, Paul shows us that people cannot take the place of God. People will let us down. God will not. We must embrace the realm of God— centering our lives wholly on Christ (2 Cor 6:15–16; 7:1).

> People will let us down. God will not.

Paul stands in awe of the God who comforts, the God who raises the dead, the God who delivers (2 Cor 1:3, 9–10). He calls the Corinthians to join with him in praise, so that when thanks is given for God's deliverance, it may be given by many (2 Cor 1:11). Pain is not meant to be endured alone—especially not pain for the sake of the gospel. Instead, pain is communal. We all support one another in it. This is the distinctly Christian way; anything less falls short of God's intentions. When pain is then triumphed over, we can all praise God together. God's victories are the victories of all of us.

Triumph over pain and despair is exactly what God wants for our lives. He believes that we can overcome;

in fact, he enables us to do so through the power of Christ. God believes in you so much that he sent his only Son to die for you (John 3:16–17). Who believes in you more than that? That's a God I can believe in—one who believes that I can be more than my pain. That's a God *you* can believe in too; he is a God you can put your hope and confidence in (compare 2 Cor 1:9–10).

I do not speak these words idealistically, but instead as one who understands what it means to hurt. I know what it's like to carry deep wounds—wounds so deep that, in a way, they will always be with you. But I also know the God who can use the thorns in our flesh to do great things (2 Cor 12:7–10). I know that God can use anything for his ultimate glory, and Paul knew it too.

So what do you know in your heart to be true? What ties with darkness do you need to cut?

### SUGGESTED READING

- ☐ 2 Corinthians 1:3–11
- ☐ Psalm 25
- ☐ Psalm 40

## Reflection

Are you allowing people in your life to take the place of God? Who? And how can you change the thought patterns that lead to this misplaced confidence?

_____

_____

_____

What past wounds have you experienced that you need to give to God? (It often helps to write them out.)

_____

_____

_____

What difficulties have you seen Christ overcome in your life? In what ways do these triumphs give you hope for the future?

_____

_____

_____

# DEFENDING OURSELVES LIKE PAUL WOULD

## 2 Corinthians 1:12–3:18

We're all tempted at one point or another to defend ourselves; we want to prove to the world that we're right and they're wrong. To do so, we usually cite our credentials, noting all the ways that we're qualified to handle a situation. But Paul fights against this tendency by citing a different kind of résumé. He shows us that what many people view as strength might actually be weakness, while what some call weakness could really be strength.

> What many people view as strength might actually be weakness, while what some call weakness could really be strength.

At the center of Paul's worldview is the transformative work of Christ—a work that we should not just preach about but expect to occur. We should act as if Jesus' transformative work is always occurring, in ourselves and the lives of others. And whenever we don't see transformation, we should stop to seriously question our approach to life and ministry. We should presume that the work of Christ is always happening.

## Presuming the Work of Christ

One of my professors once remarked that the Corinthian correspondence presumes the key elements of the Christ-story: Jesus' preexistence, life, death, and resurrection. With this remark, he meant that every major point Paul makes is really focused on the reality of Jesus. Paul knows that, in the end, nothing is about himself; it's all about Jesus. This same professor also remarked that God is definitively revealed in our weakness, because it shows the very power of the resurrected Christ.[1]

I desperately needed to hear these words at the time. I was struggling to hold my head up high and prove myself during my undergraduate and graduate degrees. I believed that if I just worked hard enough, for long enough, that I would make it. I believed that somehow all the inadequacies in me could be worked out as I performed perfectly, as a student and as a minister. But just like my depression was a lie that I had indulged for so long, once again I was believing in a lie: I had built into myself the feeling of self-reliance.

Depression creates self-reliance, in the sense that being depressed means deciding that your worldview of sadness is somehow the right one. The depressed person comes to believe that he or she is the only person who can see the truth about the world. The depressed person looks at the world so differently from the happy person that they think the happy person must be deceiving himself or herself.

Self-reliance and self-trust is incredibly dangerous. At one point during my undergraduate degree, I became so tense and so sleep-deprived—through depending purely on my own strength—that I had a panic attack after failing a quiz. Thinking that I was having a heart attack, I went straight to the doctor— only to discover just how powerful my brain was over my body. It was all in my head. That's when I first began to realize that I was going to fail without God, but it would take me years to really understand that truth. I went back to my dorm room and continued to work as though everything was up to me.

In 2 Corinthians, Paul shows the destructive power of a self-reliant worldview like mine. As he compares human wisdom to godly wisdom—our ways to God's ways—Paul demonstrates that living for God and with God far outweighs every other option. He tells the Corinthian believers:

> For our reason for boasting is this: the testimony of our conscience that we conducted ourselves in the world, and especially toward you, in holiness and purity of motive from God, not in merely human wisdom, but by the grace of God (2 Cor 1:12).

Paul measures the effectiveness of his work by whether his conduct is clearly set apart for God and is pure in motive. In addition, his work must be done "by the grace of God." This idea resonates with what Paul says in his letter to the Philippians:

> I know how ... to make do with little and ...
> abundance. In everything and in all things I
> have learned the secret both to be filled and
> to be hungry, both to have an abundance and
> to go without. I am able to do all things by
> the one who strengthens me (Phil 4:12–13).

Paul does not measure his work on the basis of tradi-
tional achievements: scoring high on a test, drawing a
large crowd to a worship service, or funding a capital
project. Instead, Paul measures achievement on the
basis of whether he has leaned on Christ to do Christ's
work in Christ's way.

Paul's reason for boasting, then, is ultimately the
Corinthian believers themselves—their trust in Jesus.
Likewise, any boasting that the Corinthian believers
might do is based on God's work through their colleague Paul (2 Cor 1:13). We are to boast in Christ's
work in one another—and this alone. And, oh, how
wonderful it is to hear one Christian boast about another's actions on behalf of God! It's inspiring; it's conversation worth having.

## Of Travel and God

Once Paul establishes that the only thing worth boasting about is Jesus' work, he debunks a rumor about
himself—that he is indecisive or unreliable. Based
on Paul's remarks in 2 Corinthians 1:15–24, it seems
that the Corinthians thought that Paul was not being
true to his word, because he had not made a promised
visit to Corinth. He explains that he had intended to
come to them twice—once to visit and then be sent
to Macedonia for ministry work, and then again to

visit and be sent to Judaea (2 Cor 1:16). But because of the dispute that emerged between Paul and the Corinthians during his previous visit, which was filled with sorrow, he decided to change his travel plans to avoid what likely would turn out to be *another* sorrowful visit (2 Cor 2:1–3).

But the dispute and the sorrow didn't prevent Paul from loving on the Corinthians. Sometime in between Paul's sorrowful visit and the writing of 2 Corinthians, he wrote a letter that was not preserved. In mentioning this letter, Paul shows us what it means to truly love:

> For out of great distress and anguish of heart I wrote to you through many tears, not so that you may be caused to be sad, but so that you may know the love that I have especially for you (2 Cor 2:4).

It's this sorrowful letter and the church's response to it that seems to have prompted the writing of 2 Corinthians.[2] And it's Paul's mention of his letter that shows us how to respond to difficulties with other Christians: with love, but also with boldness.[3]

## THE "SORROWFUL LETTER"

The letter that Paul refers to in 2 Corinthians 2:4 has not been preserved; he probably wrote it between the time of 1 Corinthians and 2 Corinthians. Based on references to the letter, it seems its main purpose was to encourage the Corinthians to deal with believers who were going against God's will (see 2 Cor 2:6, 9; 7:12).

## Walking through Doors

Paul's boldness does not cause him to believe that he is above reproach in the eyes of all; instead, he acknowledges the Corinthians' difficulties in understanding him and proceeds to explain himself. The strained relationship between Paul and the church isn't the only thing that has kept Paul from returning to Corinth; God's plans also played a role. Paul notes that while he was in Troas (a city in modern-day Turkey), God showed him an open door for the gospel. But since he doesn't find Titus—whom he views as a necessary partner in his effort—in Troas, he goes on to Macedonia (the northern part of modern-day Greece). This means going northwest across the Aegean Sea to Macedonia (2 Cor 2:12–13) and traveling by land south to Corinth. It is this course that significantly delays his visit to Corinth.

Paul frames his change of plans in terms of God intervening in his life. And this is precisely what each of us who claim to believe in Jesus must be ready for. The thought of following God's new direction inspires Paul to insert a statement of praise:

> But thanks be to God, who always leads us in triumphal procession in Christ, and who reveals the fragrance of the knowledge of him through us in every place. For we are the aroma of Christ to God among those who are being saved and among those who are perishing, to those on the one hand an odor from death to death, and to those on the other hand a fragrance from life to life (2 Cor 2:14–16).

## Paul's Second Missionary Journey[4]

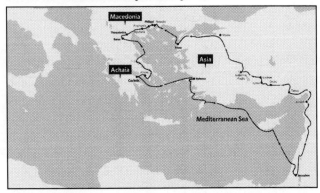

## Paul's Third Missionary Journey[5]

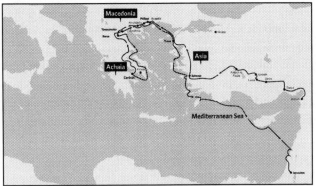

Paul lives his life with the knowledge that his calling is to represent Jesus like a wonderful fragrance—but this fragrance is not pleasing to those who reject Jesus. Here Paul clarifies his Christ-centered worldview once more: There are those who live in the life of Jesus and those who are perishing in the realm of Satan.

Although sometimes we would like to act as if it's not the case, life and death are at stake in ministry. And it's this reality that prompts Paul to say that he is no peddler of the Word of God; instead, he speaks before God himself, in Christ (2 Cor 2:16–17). He is living in the reality that his work is about life and death, and it is in the very court of God that Paul interacts. Despite opposition from the Corinthians, Paul knows the purity of his mission and he believes in the work God is doing through him—even when others (like the Corinthians) do not.

## What's a Reference Letter Worth, Anyway?

To see how God has worked through Paul's ministry, the Corinthians need to look no further than themselves, he says. He doesn't need a reference letter to prove his value; his "adequacy" comes from God, and the Corinthian believers are a living testimony of that (2 Cor 3:1–5). It's the spirit of God working among them that will grant them life, not the false peddlers of God's word (2 Cor 2:17; 3:6).

> Only God can take the darkness in our hearts and replace it with light. Only he can help us to see the world as he sees it—in the beautiful colors of redemption.

It's easy to be deceived, but when we are following Christ with everything we have, it's much harder for Satan to find a stronghold. Paul shows that our lives must be completely grounded in the work of the new covenant of Jesus (2 Cor 3:6). It provides the safety measure we're looking for—and so much more. The new covenant under Jesus has the power to save us. God is the only one who has the power to give us what we need. God is the only one who can make us sufficient for his ministry. On our own, we will always find ourselves lacking. In self-reliance, we will lose sight of the truth of the new covenant. And the truth is that only God can change the very fabric of our souls. Only God can take the darkness in our hearts and replace it with light. Only he can help us to see the world as he sees it—in the beautiful colors of redemption. Paul states this eloquently when he says:

> Not that we are adequate in ourselves to consider anything as from ourselves, but our adequacy is from God, who also makes us adequate as servants of a new covenant, not of the letter, but of the Spirit, for the letter kills, but the Spirit gives life (2 Cor 3:5-6).

Paul's relationship with the Corinthians has hope of being restored only because of Jesus. Only when Jesus is the driving force behind our discussions, and only when God's very work and person is the center of our lives, can we truly be changed. Jesus has established a new reality on earth—and, if we let it, that reality has the potential to transform all of our relationships with God's love and peace.

Because of the new covenant, Paul takes on the strength of Christ and shows the Corinthians a hopeful way forward. Their friendship can be rebuilt, but this rebuilding must be done on the basis of Jesus himself. Paul believes that he and the Corinthians can go on together, but the terms of their relationship must change to reflect the new covenant with Jesus.

Many people mistakenly assume that being a Christian means simply accepting everyone as they are, with little regard for the health of the relationship or the spiritual health of the person. Paul's actions show that he rejects this idea (2 Cor 2:5–11; compare 1 Cor 5:1–6:11). Later in the letter it becomes clear that Paul recognizes his relationship with the Corinthians as toxic, and he refuses to leave it as-is (2 Cor 13:1–10). He responds in love, but he also responds with boldness. Paul isn't afraid to speak the truth, even when the truth might hurt (2 Cor 12:21). True love doesn't let things stand where they are; true love compels relationships to move forward. Another way to put this: "[R]eal love is not afraid to bleed."[6]

> True love doesn't let things stand where they are; true love compels relationships to move forward.

Like Paul, we have to recognize when our relationships require boldness and truth. Out of love, we have to take the risky path of honest confrontation. We must count up the cost for Jesus, decide that he is worth it, and then be willing to make the tough calls. We must be willing to bleed for Christ, because he is worth everything.[7]

## Confronting Falsehoods with Jesus' Reality

We might be tempted to place our faith in things that appear to be glorious—money, careers, vacations, accomplishments—but in the end, we find that any glory from such sources is fleeting, while the glory of Christ and the Spirit overflows and endures (2 Cor 3:7–11). The Spirit gives life and sets people free; it transforms believers into the image of Christ (2 Cor 3:6, 17–18).

It is the hope of this all-surpassing glory that gives Paul boldness and prompts him to speak the truth no matter what (2 Cor 3:12).

To illustrate his point, Paul shows the Corinthians that their actions have a direct parallel in how some people in his day understood the Jewish law.[8] They clung to the law, as if it would save them, when it actually was blinding them to the truth of Jesus, who is the very fulfillment of the law (2 Cor 3:6-7, 13-17).[9] Similarly, the Corinthians—placing their hope in false leaders—have lost sight of the freedom of Jesus. Many of us today do the same. We look to leaders to draw us closer to Jesus, when we should be looking to Jesus instead. Leaders are meant to point us to Jesus, not to be some sort of substitute for him.[10]

The only reference letter worth having is a life lived for Jesus—a life that results in the lives of others being radically altered by the living Christ. As we learn to live this way, we will become truly human—as people in God's image. Paul says it this way:

> And we all, with unveiled face, reflecting
> the glory of the Lord, are being transformed
> into the same image from glory into glory,
> just as from the Lord, the Spirit (2 Cor 3:18).

The only achievement worth having is becoming more like God, via our relationship with Jesus and the working of the Holy Spirit (Phil 3:7-9). The only strength that matters is the strength rooted in God's glory—in his ability to move us from darkness to light. The only defense worth having is the reality of Christ's redemption of our lives. The only identity worth possessing is our identity as children of God, transformed into his image and reflecting his glory to the world.

> **SUGGESTED READING**
> ☐ 2 Corinthians 1:12–2:4
> ☐ 2 Corinthians 2:12–3:18
> ☐ Genesis 1:26–31
> ☐ Philippians 4:10–14

## Reflection

What are you not ready to give for Jesus yet?

_____

_____

_____

What areas of your life is God working on now—to help you better reflect his image?

_____

_____

_____

# ZEBRAS, LIONS, AND THEOLOGY

## 2 Corinthians 2:9–11

Paul's relationship with the Corinthians is complicated, to say the least. It's full of ambiguity, just like many of our relationships. But Paul's words in 2 Corinthians show that he has a general approach—a worldview. This worldview is centered on Jesus and sets everything in Paul's life in motion, including how he speaks to the Corinthians. Paul's worldview is radically life-altering; this becomes obvious when we place his words in 2 Corinthians against the backdrop of 1 Corinthians.

## Satan and the Messiness at Corinth

In 1 Corinthians (which is really Paul's second letter to the Corinthian church), he addresses all sorts of spiritual issues that could compromise the effectiveness of God's work among the Corinthians. Paul focuses on how the believers should interact with culture, deal with sin in their community, and conduct their worship services. Upon reading Paul's strong rebuke, we would expect the Corinthian believers to repent, but their response seems to be quite different.

Second Corinthians shows us that there are still problems among the Corinthian believers over the same spiritual issues Paul addressed in 1 Corinthians and likely in his third letter (the sorrowful letter mentioned in 2 Cor 2:3–4; 7:8, 12). And in fact, the issues are heightened: As we learn later in 2 Corinthians, false apostles are attracting followers in Corinth and undermining Paul's authority (2 Cor 11:3–4, 12–13). With this background in mind, we expect Paul's response to be one of absolute fury. Instead, he writes to the Corinthians with compassion, even while he addresses the tough issues firmly and boldly.

At the center of all of these emotions—and the Corinthian mess in general—are relationships. Relationships are at the center of everything we do, regardless of whether we like that to be the case. No life is built without the incredible influence of other people. Relationships make us both better and worse people. We are always given a choice about how we react, but the reality of the world's effect

> Relationships are at the center of everything we do, regardless of whether we like that to be the case.

on us is inevitable. The question is: Will we make the world better before it makes us worse? It is this same idea that drives Paul's words to the Corinthians.

Paul could view the messy relationships in Corinth purely as a source of pain—and then either walk away or respond in anger. Instead, he responds with deep love. He decides that he will change the world rather than let the world change him. This is most profoundly seen in 2 Corinthians 2, when Paul says that he wrote:

> In order that I could know your proven character, whether you are obedient in everything. Now to whomever you forgive anything, I also do; for indeed, whatever I have forgiven, if I have forgiven anything, it is for your sake in the presence of Christ, in order that we may not be exploited by Satan (for we are not ignorant of his schemes) (2 Cor 2:9–11).

Paul writes for more than himself; he writes to see the lives of others changed. He writes to bring about forgiveness. Paul writes to ensure that he, Timothy, and the Corinthian believers are not exploited by Satan. Paul understands the schemes of Satan and thus makes every effort to avoid falling into them.

What Paul says here is even more profound if the person he is forgiving in 2 Corinthians 2 is the same man "cast to Satan" in 1 Corinthians 5—a man who was committing a sickening sexual sin:

> It is reported everywhere that there is sexual immorality among you, and sexual immorality of such a kind which does not even exist among [non-Jewish people], so that someone has the wife of his father. And you are inflated with pride, and should you not rather have mourned, so that the one who has done this deed would be removed from your midst? … I have already passed

judgment on the one who has done this. ...
In the name of our Lord Jesus, when you are
assembled ... together with the power of our
Lord Jesus, hand over such a person to Satan
for the destruction of the flesh, in order that
his spirit may be saved in the day of the Lord
(1 Cor 5:4–5).[1]

The man Paul talks about in 1 Corinthians is likely
refusing to repent from his sin, and thus cheapening
the grace of Jesus—setting a bad example for other
believers.[2] He also taints the reputation of Christians
in general in Corinth, since he was committing sins
that even the Roman Empire objected to—having sex,
likely regularly, with his mother or stepmother. This
type of sin results in the man being excluded from
the Corinthian community—meaning their worship
gatherings, meals, and the Lord's Supper.

### A COMMON THEME OF RECONCILIATION

The Corinthian believers may have been worried
they had upset Paul by forgiving the man mentioned
in 2 Corinthians 2:10 (especially if this man is the
same one mentioned in 1 Cor 5:1–13). But Paul
makes it clear that he is not upset and, in fact,
supports their reconciliation as long as the sanctity
of the church is upheld. In several of his letters,
Paul encourages believers to forgive one another,
strengthening the church in unity (see Eph 4:32;
2 Cor 5:18; Col 3:13).

No matter which way we read 1 Corinthians
5:1–5, it's clear that for Paul you are either in God's

community—his Church—or under Satan's reign. It seems that any decision to not enter into God's protection leaves a person vulnerable to Satan's power. This is a worldview that is lost on our culture today. There is only one way to be saved, and that's through relationship with Jesus—which by necessity involves repentance from sins.

I am not arguing for harder lines here around our churches, or for any type of new fundamentalism; I am opposed to such ideas. But we do need to understand the basic difference between a person who knows Jesus and one who does not. We simply cannot expect for someone who does not know Jesus to act like someone who does. Likewise, we cannot expect such a person to draw us closer to God's ways or to give us godly wisdom.

On the other hand, we must expect people who *do* know Jesus to live in faithful obedience to him (1 Cor 5:9–13; Rom 6:1–7, 17–19). The idea that it's the church's job to simply allow everybody to be whoever they are and do whatever they want does not align with God's redemptive purposes. We should always make room in our church for people who do not know Jesus, but someone who claims to know Jesus and chooses to live a life of utter sin must be held accountable. If this person goes one step further toward committing actions that are causing the church's reputation to be harmed, or is making the church unsafe for others, then the church should ask that person to leave.

When we embrace someone who claims to know Jesus but we don't expect them to be obedient to him, we are undermining the very gospel we claim to believe in—a gospel that transforms and heals and brings new creation. There are certain rare occasions when people need to be asked to leave Christian communities, and—like the man Paul casts to Satan in 1 Corinthians 5:1–15—this approach will ultimately be better for them and the church.

If the man Paul forgives in 2 Corinthians 2:10 is the same man who was cast to Satan in 1 Corinthians 5:5, then we have direct evidence of the effectiveness of Paul's approach. Ultimately, the man repented and could be invited back into the Christian community and forgiven. And even if these passages are about two different people, we see in 2 Corinthians that forgiveness can happen even in extremely difficult circumstances. In the love of Christ, broken relationships can be reconciled, and they *should* be.

## Of Satan, Lions, and Hyenas

The language about Satan's schemes in 2 Corinthians 2:11 reminds us that people outside the Church truly are vulnerable. There was a time when I didn't understand the reality of God's realm and Satan's realm. Back then, I believed in the Church being "always a place for you"—as the coffee cups read in the megachurch I grew up in. And, in the process of believing this, I nearly found myself without a place to belong.

When I was 18, I started a ministry with a few friends. It was a Friday-night evangelical event—a coffee house we set up in a church that was really a dance hall. We thought we had a chance to create something big and incredible for young adults—an alternative to partying in a college town—and we hoped that it would bring lots of people to Jesus. We had some success, but it was different from what we anticipated. Before we knew it, our coffee-house ministry had become a small church in a way, with people ages 7 to 70. Some needed healing from previous church experiences, and others had never been to church in their life. All of them were looking to learn about Jesus and go deeper in their faith.

God did some pretty amazing things, like bring an ex-gang leader to Jesus, serve a dying man in his last days, and drill six water wells in an impoverished part of India. But I wasn't ready to be a pastor; I still had lots of perpetual sins to work through. I was only 19 when our ministry was rapidly expanding, and I had few leaders who could take over my responsibilities. At the same time, I was balancing my undergraduate studies, which required learning two ancient languages at once, and a part-time job as a drafter.

Desperate for help, I appointed the wrong person to leadership. He turned out to be a lion in the clothing of a gazelle. He seemed like a repentant sinner who was eager to help, with lots of time on his hands. But time was one of his main problems—he was hiding a drug problem, a criminal record, a history of mental instability, and demonic possession. He passed his time by indulging his habits. You can see where this story is going—he grew closer to me and slowly poisoned my mind like Gríma Wormtongue does to King Théoden in *The Two Towers*. And like Théoden, I allowed it to happen, indulging his comments because they appealed to my ego and insecurities.[3]

Eventually, the truth about my Gríma came out when he went crazy, revealing his possession during a prayer meeting. I wasn't at that gathering, but it traumatized those who were there. This mistake nearly ended my ministry—and it took me years to recover.

But it wasn't just trauma that our Gríma inflicted on our community. He also shook the faith of those involved. I painfully watched the weaker people who had experienced this traumatizing event get picked off by what I call spiritual "hyenas." Spiritual hyenas usually come in the form of addiction to things that are legal in most places (like alcoholism or viewing of pornography), but really are coping mechanisms that hurt the user and others far more than the user realizes (compare 2 Cor 12:20–21). Hyenas also come in the form of toxic friendships, business relationships, or dating relationships. When people become "unequally yoked," as Paul calls it, they are likely to lose their way (2 Cor 6:14).

If Satan is like a ravaging lion, then the hyenas are evil spirits and people who prey on the weak, assuring that their chances of recovery are minimal (1 Pet 5:8). I attempted to stop the spiritual hyenas by surrounding the people with love and strong friends and by warning them of the danger, but my attempts were unsuccessful.

> If Satan is like a ravaging lion, then the hyenas are evil spirits and people who prey on the weak, assuring that their chances of recovery are minimal.

The reason for all my failings is quite clear in retrospect. I had personal problems and wasn't fit to lead; I needed to mature as a leader and as a Christian. I was arrogant, still working through my own faith struggles, and falling into regular sin patterns. Early on, I should have realized this and handed off the ministry to someone else, but I lacked the humility to do so. It's this same lack of humility that resulted in the Corinthian believers being led astray (see 1 Cor 5:2; compare 2 Cor 10:5; 12:20).

But it's also important for ministers to realize that sometimes all they can do for a person is warn them, and then if the person refuses to change—and is causing harm—to dismiss them (e.g., 1 Cor 5:1–5). As things stand today, I'm extremely cautious about the people I let get close to me and influence me. I'm also engaged in intensive accountability, about absolutely everything in my personal and professional life, to ensure that I am fit to lead, in or out of season (on the clock or off the clock). Ultimately, all this comes down to growing close to Christ and doing whatever it takes to ensure that your relationships and those of the people you're leading are becoming more centered on him. Will you still fail? At times, I'm sure you will—and I know that I do—but the response rate to failure and recovery time is much faster.

## African Landscapes and God at Work

We often make poor decisions because we are usually left to make them in the shadows. Hindsight is simply that—hindsight. We don't have the advantage of hindsight when events are in process. There are many who would like to say that good and evil can be clearly distinguished, but Paul shows that the world is much more complicated than this: Lions can look like gazelles, and hyenas can look like zebras.

The whole problem makes me think of the dilemma of an early aviator in Africa. In *West with the Night*,

Beryl Markham tells of attempting to spot elephants from a plane. She describes how when hunters first spotted elephants from a plane, the animals would simply scatter in all directions—until they figured out that planes were the makings of people. The elephants then started hiding their males in the middle of the pack, so that hunters could not see their tusks. Eventually, the elephants got even smarter and would stick their heads in trees when planes came by— inevitably leading Markham to land the plane only to discover a female elephant with her head in the tree. Elephants, out of self- (and pack-) preservation, know how to deceive and pretend. Why would we be so ignorant as to think that people will not do the same? But unlike elephants, predators don't just hide; they hunt in the shadows.

Elsewhere in the book, Markham tells the story of nearly dying after a lion snuck up on her as a kid. You never know where a lion will come from or how it will hide. Satan is the same way. As Peter says, "Your adversary the devil walks around like a roaring lion, looking for someone to devour" (1 Pet 5:8).

Over time, Markham's senses heightened. She became one with each landscape she visited and moved to; she adapted. She learned how to distinguish between truth and falsehood from a plane. She acted on her instincts, and doing so often led to her survival.[4]

We each must learn to see things as they actually are, even when we can only see shapes from an elevated view. We must recognize lions for what they are. We must also recognize when it is appropriate to offer acceptance back into the Christian community— when someone is safe and when they are not.

In the case of my Gríma, it's difficult to imagine how he could be welcomed into a Christian community that I'm part of—and I have made sure that he is not welcome where I am. But I also have friends who have betrayed my trust and hurt me, but who have later repented. Then I have welcomed them back into my life; these are safe people who simply made mistakes.[5]

In the case of the man Paul forgives in 2 Corinthians, it's clear that the community has evaluated him and determined that he could be welcomed back in. We have to operate on a case-by-case basis, but we must do so with discernment. We must be unafraid to do what is necessary for the well-being of our communities. We must be forgiving, but we also must realize that loving others means making intelligent decisions. At times, loving people means cutting ties with someone in our church who knowingly embraces darkness.

> We must be forgiving, but we also must realize that loving others means making intelligent decisions.

**SUGGESTED READING**

- [ ] 2 Corinthians 2:9–11
- [ ] 1 Corinthians 5:1–12
- [ ] 1 Peter 5:8–11

## Reflection

What past relationships did you fail to end that caused you unnecessary future pain?

_____

_____

_____

What type of discernment strategy can you put in place?

_____

_____

_____

# WHO DO YOU WORK FOR—REALLY?

## 2 Corinthians 4:1–6:13

Jesus wants us to discover how to live life fully—as people living in God's image for his purposes. Everything we do should be about the aims of the living God, who is teaching us how to truly live. Yet, this often is not the case; we separate and compartmentalize our lives.[1] We draw lines between our lives at church, work, and home. In reality, God wants to work in all parts of our lives.

> God wants to work in all parts of our lives. He sees no division between who we are in one place and who we are in another.

He sees no division between who we are in one place and who we are in another. He wants us to live authentically for him everywhere, in every situation.

## Truth Leads to Authentic Change

Truth leads us to openness with our lives; it opens up the reality that is God's. Paul tells the Corinthian believers that since God has shown him great mercy, he refuses to lose heart or exploit the Word of God (2 Cor 4:1–2). Instead, Paul practices his ministry with transparency (2 Cor 4:3). Thus, if the Corinthian believers seek clarity from Paul, then they should understand that whenever he seems unclear, it is because they are blinded by the work of evil—the god of this age, Satan.[2] Paul's ministry is completely centered in the work of Christ, so any lack of clarity is not an issue with his words, but with the people receiving the message; some people are blind to the truth of what Paul is saying.

What Paul means by his "god of this age" language is not that Satan rules the world in this age, but that the priorities of this age—rather than God—often rule over people's lives. Satan can use things like idolatry—whether that be physical idols we worship or the god of money—to control us and manipulate us. This blinds us to God's truth. When the Corinthian believers buy into the practices of the larger culture at Corinth—such as idolatry, or the values of the false apostles, like charisma—they lose sight of the truth. And in losing sight of the truth, they lose sight of who Paul is.

And this returns to Paul's overall point in 2 Corinthians: Satan aims to blind us and will use any and all means necessary. We must live in the light of the good news of Jesus—in Jesus' realm instead of in Satan's. And we must do whatever is necessary to ensure that we continue to live in Christ. But this effort must be balanced with the work of spreading the gospel; we must be in the world, but not of it (John 17:14–16). We must live for Jesus, as his ambassadors (like Paul), extending the reach of the gospel and bringing God's vibrant light to our communities and world. This is how we push back the darkness and help people find victory over the god of this age.

It is Christ himself who is the glory of God—his very image. It is Christ who can bring us into the spectrum and beauty of God's light. If we settle for anything less, we will simply be living in blindness (2 Cor 4:4). It's because of this very sentiment that Paul can say: "For we do not proclaim ourselves, but Christ Jesus as Lord, and ourselves as your slaves for the sake of Jesus" (2 Cor 4:5). Whenever we seek to promote ourselves instead of Jesus, we lose sight of God's intended purposes. If our work, or anything in life for that matter, becomes about us instead of God, we are drifting away from the realm of Christ. We are mere servants of God, bearing his image through the power of Jesus—nothing more, nothing less. God wishes to shine in our lives, so that the world may be transformed into beauty, so that the sin and darkness may be pushed away as God takes over:

> For God who said, "Light will shine out of darkness," is the one who has shined in our hearts for the enlightenment of the knowledge of the glory of God in the face of Christ. But we have this treasure in earthenware jars, in order that the extraordinary degree of the power may be from God and not from us (2 Cor 4:6–7).

The only enlightenment worth having and embracing is that which belongs to God. There is no separation in Paul's thought between the various parts of our lives. God wants *all* of our lives. We cannot rule one part and expect Christ to reign in the rest. Christ must have it all. That is the only path that can lead to true transformation—the only path that brings the wonderment of salvation to the here and now.

> ### THE IMAGE OF GOD
>
> In 2 Corinthians 4:4 Paul refers to Jesus as the "image of God" (and again in Col 1:15; compare Phil 2:6). The same phrase also appears in Genesis 1:26–27; 5:1–3; 9:6.

## What the Gospel Requires

The gospel will require everything of us. You can't desire to be as effective as Paul without also being willing to suffer for Jesus (2 Cor 4:8–9). We must "always carry ... around the death of Jesus in our body, in order that the life of Jesus may also be revealed" (2 Cor 4:10). When we advocate on behalf of Christ's salvation, even at great cost to ourselves, we show others who Jesus truly is—and furthermore, we give God a chance to mold us into people who live according to his image (2 Cor 4:11–13). But we are not alone in this. We serve the resurrected Jesus, who will also raise us up with him (2 Cor 4:14).

> We cannot rule one part [of our lives] and expect Christ to reign in the rest. Christ must have it all.

As we reflect God's image, we take on the appearance of the Suffering Servant, who died and rose again for us (Isa 53:10–12). We begin to be like Jesus, willing to suffer and die for others—knowing that with each small death of ourselves we find life in Christ. In the process, we show the world that true power looks like weakness, but it is strength in the living God. Like Paul, we begin to embrace the idea, "Blessed are the meek, because they will inherit the earth" (Matt 5:5). We know that when we suffer for others, it is gain for the gospel. We know that we serve the victorious one who is Christ—so no matter what hardships and afflictions may come our way, God will have victory over them.

> With each small death of ourselves we find life in Christ. In the process, we show the world that true power looks like weakness, but it is strength in the living God.

It is a sad thing that we don't embrace the full story of the gospel—the one that requires everything of us—because no great story has ever been written that did not contain conflict. No great character was ever made who did not face extreme trial. And the same is true for the Christian.[3] We cannot be made into who we are meant to be without difficulty (2 Cor 4:15–17). It is through conflict that God builds his eternal strength and hope in us. It is through conflict that we find out who we are. When all of our façades are stripped away by hardship, we see the person underneath; we see whether our lives are truly and fully devoted to God; we see the temporary fall away as the eternal takes over through the power of Christ (2 Cor 4:18).

## The Struggle of Being Human

It is understandable that this life is a struggle—with obligations, occupations, and the constant back-and-forth of becoming better than we are. Paul tells us that we feel the tension of life because we live now in a "tent," an "earthly house," but we long to put on the "dwelling from heaven" (2 Cor 5:1–2). Until that day of transformation comes, we have to deal with the limits of being human. Will we let the desires of this world, which embraces the temporary and fleeting, rule over us? Will we let the "god of this age" reign in our lives? Or will we instead seek the eternal, where we have a perpetual dwelling with God himself? Will we embrace what it means to be truly human in the kingdom of God, or will we chase after the sad definition of humanity that Satan's realm offers to us?

When Paul speaks about these temporary tents we live in, he speaks as someone well acquainted with the metaphor, since making tents was his occupation while he lived in Corinth (Acts 18:1–3). Paul knows that work itself is meant to be completely infiltrated by God's presence. He worked during his time in Corinth—refusing to rely on the church for his material needs—so that his message would be pure and his motives clear (2 Cor 11:7–9; 1 Cor 4:11–13).

Paul says that we already have the "down payment" of what is to come—the Spirit (2 Cor 5:5). We have God living in our tents, showing us the way forward. This Spirit offers us the promise of something better: to be absent from these tents and with the God we love (2 Cor 5:6–8). But this doesn't mean that we should despise the tents we live in here and now. Instead, we should aim to please God in everything we do (2 Cor 5:9; compare 2 Cor 6:16). It is through the Spirit that we live now for God, in relationship with him. The justice of God, his judgment, is coming to all (2 Cor 5:10). We will all be held accountable before him, so the question is: What will we do in light of that reality? Will we live for him, or will we throw away the beautiful gift of life that we have here on earth?

## Do You Fear God?

The idea of the coming judgment leads into Paul's remark about "the fear of the Lord" (2 Cor 5:11). None of us wants to talk about the reality of judgment—that you either know Jesus and believe in him, leading to eternal life, or you deny him and find yourself facing death. We fear the Lord, for we know that he expects much of us. But at the same time, we realize that we can do the Lord's work only by embracing his strength. It is not that we stand and wonder what he wants, or that we work to achieve some checklist to please him; instead we embrace the salvation he offers, in wonderment at his grace, and then act according to the will of the Spirit in thankfulness of this grace.

Paul does absolutely everything with the endgame in mind, and we should do the same (2 Cor 5:11). Endgame objectives—objectives that focus on Jesus' work, conducted by his will and in his power—should be the only thing we ever boast about (2 Cor 5:12). So many of us desire to have control over our lives and destinies—ultimate autonomy. We pursue that control through wealth and through occupations. But Paul shows that autonomy is not really the final objective at all. Instead, the objective is to give complete control over to God, so that we can learn what it means to live in his image:

> For the love of Christ controls us, because we have concluded this: that one died for all; as a result all died. And he died for all, in order that those who live should no longer live for themselves, but for the one who died for them and was raised (2 Cor 5:14–15; compare 5:13).

This conclusion changes absolutely everything. Because of Christ's death and resurrection, Paul can say that he no longer judges (or regards) anyone according to the flesh—according to human standards or what they can achieve[4]—but instead judges people according to the Spirit's work within them (2 Cor 5:16). Paul explains this with the statement: "If anyone is in Christ, he is a new creation" (2 Cor 5:17).[5] The reality of Jesus so radically alters our reality that we are new creations in him and through him. The result of Jesus is new creation—and, oh, what a beautiful thing that is.

The reality of Jesus so radically alters our reality that we are new creations in him and through him. The result of Jesus is new creation—and, oh, what a beautiful thing that is.

Without Jesus, I am not able to achieve anything worth doing. I wouldn't even be able to speak correctly without him. I had a severe speech impediment until age 8. Yet at one point in my life, I lost sight of this; as I stacked up achievements from my occupation, the humility of my undergraduate work (and the accompanying panic attacks) went away and was replaced by arrogance. The arrogance was a falsehood; it masked the truth that I was insecure in who I was. No matter how many achievements I stacked up, I still felt the need to defend myself and prove myself. I felt the need to take credit for everything I touched. But Jesus was the one doing it all. He was the only one who rightfully deserved credit. And what did it matter anyway, if it wasn't about his end goal?

There was darkness in my heart that I had to cut ties with. The only way to do so was to become transparent with everyone around me, to apologize to them for my arrogance, and to ask that they hold me accountable in the future. So, that's what I did. It was painful—and at times, my sincere apology was not received well. But Jesus used it nonetheless, and as I gradually let Christ work in me again, I began to once again give him credit. I let the compartmentalization of my job from the rest of my life be reduced to ashes, and I embraced the resurrected life of Jesus instead. And, oh, was it freeing. Suddenly I could be who God intended me to be.

Paul summarizes the shift that occurs in a true believer in Jesus when he says: "[T]he old has passed away; behold, new has come" (2 Cor 5:17).[6] All of this happens because of the reconciliation between us and God the Father that Jesus has made possible (2 Cor 5:18). Like Paul, it is our job to call others to this same reconciliation—to living fully for Jesus (2 Cor 5:20). Paul explains the message of Jesus beautifully and wonderfully when he says:

> God was in Christ reconciling the world
> to himself, not counting their trespasses

against them. ... We beg you on behalf of
Christ, be reconciled to God. He made the
one who did not know sin to be sin on our
behalf, in order that we could become the
righteousness of God in him (2 Cor 5:19, 21).

## Working as Ambassadors for Christ

As "ambassadors" of Christ, we are meant to be people
who proclaim this message everywhere—who speak
it in boldness and with truth (2 Cor 5:20). Like Paul,
we are to say to the people we meet, "We beg you on
behalf of Christ, be reconciled to God," urging them
"not to receive the grace of God in vain" (2 Cor 5:20;
6:1). It is not just that Jesus has achieved great things
for us, but that we are to respond by acting like this reality really does change everything—because it does.

Our daily actions reflect who we really work for:
Do we work for the living God, or do we live like we're
part of the realm of Satan? Paul does not embrace the
work of the world, but instead highlights all of his difficulties on behalf of Jesus to show that the work of God
is indeed real in him. He does not do his work seeking
achievements of this world, but instead for heaven-
ly purposes (2 Cor 6:3-10).
As a result of all of this, Paul
asks the Corinthians to be
open to an authentic relationship with Jesus once more
(2 Cor 6:11-13). Paul's heart is
open wide for such a relationship, but it's clear to him that
the Corinthians are not quite

God is confronting
us with who we are
... but we refuse to
give into him and
his ways. We let
ourselves fall into
the same old habits
and darkness.

ready for it yet. And isn't the same thing true for many of us? God is confronting us with who we are—with our arrogance, anxiety, and depression, and with the strongholds of sin left in our lives—but we refuse to give into him and his ways. We let ourselves fall into the same old habits and darkness.

The darkness can be pushed back by the work of the living light that is Jesus if we will simply be open to it.

### SUGGESTED READING

- ☐ 2 Corinthians 4:1–6:13
- ☐ 1 Peter 5:1–11

## Reflection

What areas of your life are still ruled by "the god of this age"? What can you do to hand them over to Christ's reign instead?

_____

_____

_____

What are some practical things you can do to help others center their lives on Christ—and find freedom in his power?

_____

_____

# JOY, GRIEF, AND MAKING PEACE

## 2 Corinthians 7:2-16

The natural result of living in Christ's realm is that we enjoy his world. When we commit to Jesus' realm—to his way of living—we see all the possibilities. We see how Jesus' light can change the darkness,[1] how the spectrum of his light, like colors of a rainbow, is at work in our world. Once we see the possibilities of God's work, we realize that our world could be a better place. And our natural inclination should be to make it a better place—to take action on behalf of Christ. This action starts in us. As our spirit changes to be more like the image of God, so do the actions of our flesh. It's with these ideas in mind that Paul opens the seventh chapter of 2 Corinthians.

## Making Room in Our Hearts

Continuing with the thought that we must separate from all that defiles God's work, including toxic relationships, Paul says: "Make room for us [Paul and Timothy] in your hearts ... I have already said that you are in our hearts, so that we die together and we live together" (2 Cor 7:2–3). Here we see that, despite all of Paul's difficulties with the Corinthians, he still regularly boasts about them (2 Cor 7:4). Paul is a master pastor with deep affection for the church he planted. This affection causes him to be proud of them, like a father would be proud of his kids carrying on his legacy; but also, since he is like a father to them, he knows that they can be more and do more for Christ than they are doing now.

Paul may have joy in his affliction as a missionary, but he still desires the support of the Corinthian community (2 Cor 7:4). And it's with this that we get a glimpse into what it's really like to be Paul. The door may have been open to him to minister in Macedonia—to spread the good news of Jesus there—but it was still deeply trying. He experienced "quarrels outside" and "fears within" (2 Cor 7:5). But God always delivers. He gives us just what we need, just in time. For Paul, this meant Titus joining him and Timothy (2 Cor 7:6).[2]

It's difficult to imagine this incredible point in history: Here in Macedonia, we have Paul and the two men he invested the most in—Timothy and Titus—all ministering together. This is a powerhouse team for God's kingdom. We also see just how much ministry Paul shared in common with those whom he mentored. Paul says that Titus reported the Corinthian believers' "longing ... mourning ... and zeal for [Paul]," leading him to "rejoice even more" (2 Cor 7:7). At this point, we learn that Paul and the Corinthian believers were beginning to see eye to eye by the time he wrote 2 Corinthians, but there were still some important details left to work through.

## Grief That's Worth It

The details in our relationships are often the things that are most painstaking. At times, it seems easier to ignore them for the sake of "keeping the peace." Yet, Jesus says, "Blessed are the peacemakers" (Matt 5:9). Notice that he doesn't say, "Blessed are the peace-keepers." Making peace requires action, and at times those actions are very painful; they require incredibly difficult decisions. For Paul, this decision was to send his sorrowful letter to the Corinthians—and we can only imagine all the anxiety that he would have had after doing so. But ultimately, Paul felt called to send the letter because it was a letter of peacemaking. Jesus' kind of peace, built on the sturdy ground of God's ways, is the only kind worth having. Paul says:

> If indeed I grieved you by my letter, I do not regret it. Even if I did regret it (I see that that letter grieved you, even though for a short time), now I rejoice, not that you were grieved, but that you were grieved to repentance. For you were grieved according to the will of God, so that you suffered loss in no way through us. For grief according to the will of God brings about a repentance leading to salvation, not to be regretted, but worldly grief brings about death (2 Cor 7:8–10).

Not all grief is a bad thing; grief from God that brings about a real change in our hearts and actions is well worth it. It is a passing grief that leads to transformation. It means cutting ties with darkness and walking in the light with Jesus instead.

Because of the change the Corinthians made as a result of Paul's letter, he regards them as innocent—just as Jesus himself would regard them (2 Cor 7:11). This is not Paul saying that the Corinthian believers did no wrong, for indeed they made a mistake; instead, Paul is acknowledging their state before Christ—and thus himself—as people who are repentant and thus free from the previous sin (2 Cor 7:11-12). In other words, what separates us from sin is not time, but the love of God. For people who repent, their sin is as far as the east is from the west—infinitely separated (Psa 103:12).

The natural result of living separated from sin is hospitality and love. It's seeing the mutual connection between us and others—we all are people who desperately need the love of God and the salvation of his Son, Jesus Christ. This is the precise response the Corinthians had when Titus visited them: They "refreshed" his spirit (2 Cor 7:13-16).

> The natural result of living separated from sin is hospitality and love.

The Corinthian response to Paul's rebuke was so godly that it leads Paul to say: "I rejoice, because in everything I am completely confident in you" (2 Cor 7:16).

At this point, we may be wondering, "What, then, is Paul writing about? It seems that all is well." But this is again where Paul shows us his heart. He can rejoice at one change in the Corinthian believers while still expecting more of them. And this is how each of us should feel as we lead others close to Jesus—we should be filled with joy when their lives align with God's expectations but recognize that they can do more.

## Chasing Rainbows and Making Peace

When we're in the process of dealing with difficult relationships, we have to be able to see the good in others. If we simply look for what needs to be corrected, we will not be able to make peace.

In Paul's kind remarks to the Corinthian believers, he shows us that there are many ways to look at God's light. The Corinthian believers—or some of them, at least—are on the verge of stepping into the realm of Satan, away from God's light. At the same time, Paul affirms the beautiful work that Christ is doing in them. Paul sees the beautiful colors of God at work among them. He recognizes God in them—and in that he finds a connection.

I'm betting that all of us who are Christians have felt this connection with other Christians before, even those we struggle to deal with. The connection is a bit like experiencing a rainbow with a stranger: You both stand in awe of it, wondering how this cosmic event can make both of you feel like you're the same when you're so different. Of all things, a song summarizes this well:

> Have you been half asleep?
> And have you heard voices?
> I've heard them calling my name.
> Is this the sweet sound
> That calls the young sailors?
> The voice might be one and the same.
> I've heard it too many times to ignore it,
> It's something that I'm supposed to be.
> Someday we'll find it,
> The rainbow connection,
> The lovers, the dreamers, and me.[3]

And at one point, the song says, "All of us under its spell, we know that it's probably magic." And that is what believing in Jesus is like, and the connection it creates between us. It unites us. It pushes us forward. It feels like magic. It's the sweet sound of the voice of God calling us, like a sailor is called to the sea.

As we make peace with others, we must be able to see the "rainbow connection" between us and them. For believers, we must be able to see the image of God at work in them and celebrate when the image of God takes over a part of their lives they once led themselves—or allowed Satan to lead. For those yet to know Jesus, we should see the potential of the image of God to reign in their lives; we should recognize the beautiful things in their lives that are from God—even when they themselves don't recognize those things—and prompt them to move toward all that is good, true, and wonderful, all that is God's will. We must see the colors of the light in our world and affirm it when we find it.

God's work is as colorful as an Indian street market or downtown New York City. God created the colors and every living creature—everything that is beautiful is from him. When God works, everything transforms from fallen to renewed.

God showed us how much he loves this world when he gave us the rainbow—after the flood. God brought the flood to restore humanity and creation as a type of last resort. After the flood, the rainbow is a sign of the covenant God makes with Noah:

> "My bow I have set in the clouds, and it shall
> be for a sign of the covenant between me and
> between the earth. And when I make clouds

appear over the earth the bow shall be seen in the clouds. Then I will remember my covenant that is between me and you, and between every living creature, with all flesh. And the waters of a flood will never again cause the destruction of all flesh. The bow shall be in the clouds, and I will see it, so as to remember the everlasting covenant between God and between every living creature, with all flesh that is upon the earth." And God said to Noah, "This is the sign of the covenant which I am establishing between me and all flesh that is upon the earth" (Gen 9:13–17).[4]

The story of Noah puts into perspective much of what is happening in 2 Corinthians. Evil exists and belongs to the realm of Satan, but God wants to redeem humanity. Rather than issue destruction, like he did in the time of Noah, he is redeeming humanity through the work of Jesus Christ—which also is seen in believers through the Holy Spirit working in them.[5]

### NOAH ELSEWHERE IN THE NEW TESTAMENT

Paul does not explicitly mention Noah in 2 Corinthians 7, but instead alludes to the imagery of the flood and the separation of evil. Noah and the flood are more plainly referenced in Jude 1:5; 1 Peter 3:18–20; and 2 Peter 2:4–5.

Scientifically speaking, a rainbow is light being reflected and refracted off water droplets. This is some of the most beautiful imagery in the Bible since it comes after the destruction of the earth by water. Yet the rainbow itself can be revealed only through water. The rainbow also reveals the reality of light itself. Light is not white; it's composed of colors. And just like light, God is not simplistic but multifaceted. God reflects his very image off of humanity—and humanity is at its height when we allow for this reflection to occur. The process of the Spirit of God filling our hearts, and redeeming our actions as a result, is the very process of refraction. Like light being refracted through water, God's transformative work in us reveals the reality of who we really are. As the old self is destroyed, like water destroyed the earth, something more beautiful emerges in all the colors of God.

Paul makes a similar point in 1 Corinthians 12–14, where he talks about the body of Christ having many parts—all of which are used for God's purposes. Spiritual gifts demonstrate how God is manifest in different ways to different people. Likewise, we see this in the Old Testament when God comes as a burning bush, rider on the clouds, pillar of smoke, and still, small voice (e.g., Exod 3:2; Psa 68:4; 1 Kgs 19:11–12). We also see this through the way the Old Testament is structured, with God speaking through the priests (the Law), the seers (Wisdom literature), and the prophets, and we also read about God speaking through kings. God uses different types of literature, and different types of people, in the process of explaining

> All of this shows that God is, in fact, an artist, molding his world to match his design.

who he is. All of this shows that God is, in fact, an artist, molding his world to match his design.

We must look together to the sign of the rainbow, which God gave Noah, and say: God wants to redeem. He does not want to destroy. God wants us all to live in the colors of his light, like people standing at the base of a rainbow—praising him for the salvation he has brought through his Son, Jesus, and the life we have in the Holy Spirit. I will find the "rainbow connection" between believers, dreamers, lovers of Christ, and me.

**SUGGESTED READING**
- ☐ 2 Corinthians 7:2–16
- ☐ 1 Kings 19:9–18

## Reflection

What beauty in creation inspires you—gives you hope in the God who made it?

_____

_____

_____

Think of four different people who reflect God's personality in four different ways. What does this teach you about God?

_____

_____

# HOW TO LOVE THE IMPOVERISHED

## 2 Corinthians 8:1–9:15

Loving someone is never easy. It always requires something of us, or it is not true love. In this regard, Paul expected much of the Corinthian believers. It was not enough that they repented from some sins; they needed to act as believers fully committed to the work of Jesus in the world. For Paul, this meant self-sacrifice; it meant giving; it meant loving the impoverished.

### Generosity Changes Everything

Paul tells the Corinthians about "the grace of God that has been given among the churches of Macedonia"—that even in "a great ordeal of affliction ... and [with their] extreme depth of ... poverty [they] have overflowed [in] ... generosity," to the point of choosing to give beyond their means (2 Cor 8:1–3). The Macedonian believers desired to be part of the ministry of the saints through giving, so they gave "first to the Lord" and then to Paul, Timothy, and Titus (2 Cor 8:4–5).[1] Paul presents this example of self-sacrifice to show the Corinthians that they have failed in their mission to support the Christians in Jerusalem—"the saints" that Paul mentions in 2 Corinthians 8:4 (also see Gal 2:9-10). In addition, Paul not-so-subtly observes that the Macedonian believers have contributed to the ministry of Paul and his colleagues; in doing so, Paul shows that the Corinthians have never once helped cover the cost of his services (2 Cor 11:9).

### PAUL'S THIRD MISSIONARY JOURNEY (AD 52–57)

Paul visits Galatia and Phrygia

Paul stays at Ephesus and writes 1 Corinthians

Paul visits Macedonia and writes 2 Corinthians[2]

And herein lies the great irony of so many who are unsettled. With hoarding, and a general lack of generosity, comes a highly critical spirit that is unhelpful. When we pay for something, we generally appreciate it more; but when it comes freely to us, at no personal cost, we are quick to become ungrateful and set it aside. We easily critique when we should be creating—or, at the very least, contributing. Paul wants to see the Corinthians take up the cause again of supporting the impoverished believers in Jerusalem, where the church began (2 Cor 8:6, 10-12). Paul's words about this are ones we all should remember:

> But just as you excel in everything—in faith and in speaking and in knowledge and with all diligence and in the love from us that is in

> you—so may you excel in this grace [that is
> giving] also (2 Cor 8:7).

In parallel to this thought, this exact phenomena
occurs all over the world where a handout culture exists. When people do not have to earn what is given
to them, they often set it aside or fail to take care of
it. This notion of charity is often deemed as "helping
that hurts" or "toxic charity."[3] With his not-so-sub-
tle comment about the Macedonians' support, Paul
shows that the same problem that exists in charity
can occur in ministry settings. When people don't
invest in the ministry services provided to them,
they can become ungrateful and hypercritical. In
the United States, this problem is seen in so-called
"church-hoppers" (or "church-shoppers"), who find
themselves unsatisfied with every church they attend
because they don't share in the costs of ministry. This
problem also occurs among commentators online,
who easily troll blogs to critique people at no cost to
themselves—or even to their reputations. They stand
in anonymity and critique without having to actually
be responsible for their toxic words. In biblical studies, a similar issue exists with scholars who critique
but never actually create; some people devote their
entire careers to doing so. It's much more difficult to
make something than to make fun of something. We
should be creators. If you don't like something, aim to
do something better and constructive; don't just stand
in judgment.[4]

Part of the act of creating a better world is giving.
I would go so far as to say that Christians who do not
give are going against Jesus' views; they're not acting
very Christian at all. Believers in Jesus are called to

care for the impoverished and to give so radically that it hurts. Paul tells the Corinthian believers that giving is how they prove the "genuineness" of their love (2 Cor 8:8).

Giving is one of the ways we follow the example of Jesus: Jesus, although rich—in the sense that he dwelled in heaven in the form of God—became poor for our sake. Born into the flesh, he emptied himself, taking the form of a servant, and literally lived as an impoverished man, all for the purpose of letting us share in the richness of relationship with God the Father (2 Cor 8:9; Phil 2:6–7; compare Isa 52:13–53:12). With Jesus' choice to become human came the possibility for all of us to be sons and daughters of the living God—adopted as his children (Gal 4:4–7; compare to 2 Cor 5:21).

With all this, Paul is neither trying to command the Corinthian believers to do something or to make them suffer; instead, he wants them to give out of their present abundance so that none may have need (2 Cor 8:8, 13–14). Paul even anticipates that, one day, the currently impoverished Jerusalem church might have an abundance that would be used to help the Corinthians—and this represents Paul's Christ-centered worldview. For Paul, being centered on Jesus means looking beyond the current set of events and recognizing both how we are all interconnected and how God can use those connections to transform lives. I have a need today that you help me with so that for your need tomorrow, I can help you. Paul is not promoting dependency or self-sufficiency; instead, he is proposing mutual love and compassion—a pooling of resources for the betterment of all (2 Cor 8:15).

## A Total Transformation

Paul goes on in 2 Corinthians to show us what he has already said in words: God's work is not just something that happens *in* us; it also happens *through* us—through our actions. We cannot be ethereal as Christians; we must be people of action. Paul demonstrates this point by sending not just Titus to the Corinthian believers, but also a "brother" who is famous among the churches for his ability to proclaim the

> God's work is not just something that happens *in* us; it also happens *through* us.

gospel and another whom Paul highly recommends (2 Cor 8:16, 18, 22).[5] Paul could send an ordinary assistant to pick up the Corinthians' offering for the impoverished, but instead he sends Titus—whom they know and respect—along with a famous speaker—to bless them through his words—and another friend.

Paul aims for this visit to be life-giving for everyone involved. By sending these three gifted men, he wants to turn a usual event into something wonderful.[6] Paul also goes out of his way to emphasize that the actual delivery of the Corinthians' offering will be by multiple people, not just Paul. This ensures that Paul is above reproach by both human standards and God's standards (2 Cor 8:19–21).

## A Little Rhetorical Flair

Paul is not above a little rhetoric to make sure that the Corinthians carry out the work that they began. He goes so far as to say, "It is unnecessary for me to write to you concerning [the offering] ... because I know your readiness to help, concerning which I keep on boasting to the Macedonians about you, that Achaia [the region of which Corinth was the capital] has been ready to help since last year, and your zeal has stirred up the majority of them" (2 Cor 9:1-2). Often we feel bad about emphasizing that people should follow through with their word, but we really shouldn't. Our "yes" should be our "yes," and our "no," our "no" (Matt 5:37; compare 2 Cor 1:17). We should expect the same from others.

In 2 Corinthians 9:3-5 we also learn that Paul plans to come to Corinth himself—hence his earlier remark that he would not deliver the offering alone and that the famous preacher has been traveling with him (2 Cor 8:18-19). However, some of the Macedonian believers might accompany Paul to Corinth, and he expresses concern that he might be humiliated in front of them if the Corinthians are unready to give (2 Cor 9:4). This would be an embarrassment, which Paul hopes to avoid by sending Titus and others to Corinth in advance (2 Cor 9:5).

## The Cheerful Giver

> The one who sows sparingly will also reap sparingly, and the one who sows bountifully will also reap bountifully. Each one should give as he has decided in his heart, not reluctantly or from compulsion, for God loves a cheerful giver. And God is able to cause all grace to abound to you, so that in everything at all times, because you have enough of

everything, you may overflow in every good work (2 Cor 9:6–8).

There is joy to be found in giving, if we do so with the right heart and according to what God has led us to do. But if we give because we feel like we have to do so, we're really missing the point. Giving is another type of action that leads to transformation in us. There have been many times in my life when I have seen this to be the case.

Paul goes on to discuss the blessings affiliated with giving. By using the analogy of a sower of seed, Paul first shows us that the very source of any wealth we have is God himself—we are merely distributing his wealth (2 Cor 9:9–10). Abraham Kuyper famously put it this way: "There is not a square inch in the whole domain of our human existence over which Christ, who is Sovereign over *all*, does not cry, '*Mine!*' "[7] Everything is God's; when we give, all we are doing is ensuring that his resources are used according to his purposes. We are either investing in what he has clearly identified as his investment, or we are giving over to others resources that we do not need at the moment, so that they may steward them for the work of God's kingdom. Each of these ways of giving is a type of stewardship that affirms that everything on earth is God's and not our own. We should give cheerfully because our giving is a recognition that we get to share in God's joy of getting his resources where they should go.

> There is joy to be found in giving, if we do so with the right heart and according to what God has led us to do.

Paul goes on to explain that we should not be concerned when we give, because God will provide for us what we need. He will bless those who give because he knows that they will continue to give (2 Cor 9:8, 10–11). When God gives a discerning giver more resources, he knows that they will get them where they need to go, according to his purposes.

## Replacing Criticism with Thankfulness

If our aim is to combat the hypercritical spirit that is at work within us—to offer a better alternative to our society—then we should aim to be generous. Paul tells the Corinthians that their generosity will not just combat poverty but also will result in a "thanksgiving to God" (2 Cor 9:12). Paul frames all of this in terms of the "gospel of Christ" (2 Cor 9:13). And this speaks volumes: Paul does not distinguish between "salvation" and the actions of the Christian believer. We cannot divorce true repentance, which will naturally lead to positive actions on behalf of God—including giving—from our beliefs (compare Mark 1:14–15). Beliefs require action; in fact, they demand it. And belief also sees God at work everywhere, constantly thanking him for the opportunity to be part of his work. Belief transforms us entirely. It is for this reason that Paul is grateful for the forthcoming gift of the Corinthian believers (2 Cor 9:15). This is not just about the people being helped; it's about how helping transforms the giver.

Generosity—leading to thankfulness—is a great way to cut ties with darkness in our lives. Whether it be depression, anxiety, addiction, or just a general frustration with life, serving others helps us move beyond ourselves. And in doing so, we get a chance to look at Jesus in them, to watch him overcome adversity in them, and to bring more hope to our own lives. When we're able to see how Jesus can help one person overcome, we also discover how he can help *us* overcome.

If you want to be not just redeemed but also transformed, look no further than changing how you manage your assets. Ask God how he wishes to use the resources that have been given to you to steward.

**SUGGESTED READING**

☐ 2 Corinthians 8:1–9:15

☐ Isaiah 52:13–53:12

## Reflection

Think upon what Jesus gave, for us, as a person. What are some practical things you can do to reflect more of his character?

_____

_____

How can you become more generous and give more? What can you do to free up more resources for the work of God's kingdom?

_____

_____

# FIGHTING THE SPIRITUAL WAR AGAINST DARKNESS

## 2 Corinthians 10:1–11:6

Humility is not easy to come by. And neither is authenticity. When it came to rebuilding his relationship with the Corinthians, Paul realized that there was much darkness to combat. This was no simple misunderstanding; it was about the basic value systems that govern people's lives.

## Ready for Spiritual War

Although Paul may be humble and meek when face to face with the Corinthian believers, he warns them that if things have not changed by the time he arrives, he will take necessary and firm actions (2 Cor 10:1–2, 6). Paul disputes that anyone at Corinth would say he is living according to the "flesh" when in fact:

> The weapons of [his] warfare are not merely human, but powerful to God for the tearing down of fortresses, tearing down arguments

and all pride that is raised up against
the knowledge of God, and taking every
thought captive to the obedience of Christ
(2 Cor 10:3–5).

In making this remark, Paul
clarifies once more what he
has emphasized throughout
2 Corinthians: This is not about
a merely human dispute; this is
a battle for souls. This is spiritual life and death. And Paul
knows that he is living accord-

> This is not about
> a merely human
> dispute; this is a
> battle for souls.
> This is spiritual
> life and death.

ing to God's ways—the ways of the spirit, not the
flesh[1]—and that any who are standing against him are
really opposing the work of God. The selfish actions of
the Corinthian believers demonstrate this.

God's ways empower Paul to take every thought
captive (2 Cor 10:5). They bring about transformation;
they completely change lives.

## Put Yourself to the Test

Aligning our lives according to Jesus' standards requires honesty. Paul tells the Corinthian believers
that, if he must, he will "punish all disobedience" so
that "obedience is completed" (2 Cor 10:6). By this,
Paul means that he aims to restore wholeness—Jesus'
net result—to their lives (2 Cor 10:8). To further illustrate this point, Paul reminds the Corinthian believers
that he, too, is in Christ, in addition to those at Corinth
who claim that they are (2 Cor 10:7). Essentially Paul
is saying, "Who are you to judge me?" In this regard,
Paul is unafraid to use his God-given authority once

he arrives in Corinth. If the believers there force his hand, he will act in person according to what he has said in writing (2 Cor 10:10–11).

If we are to live in God's image, we cannot look to our own image as the measure of success. Those who look to other people to define who they are will fail to see that they are failing God's test. Here's how Paul frames this idea:

> For we do not dare to classify or to compare ourselves with some who commend themselves, but … when they measure themselves by themselves and compare themselves with themselves, they show that they do not have understanding (2 Cor 10:12).[2]

It should be our goal to let the colors of God shine out from within us, not to reflect society's view of the "right" person. When we measure ourselves against the views of others—looking to them for affirmation— we neglect to look to God's ways. Instead of embracing God's ways, we substitute a poor reflection of humanity. If we are to look to anyone else for an example, it should be the person refracting God's light—living according to his image. For the Corinthian believers, this person was Paul, who had every right to call them to change their lives (2 Cor 10:13). He brought the gospel to Corinth and helped found the church, so any sort of self-defense that he must offer—which will, of course, look very different from the type of defense that others would offer—is well within the bounds of what's acceptable (2 Cor 10:14–15).

It is not Paul's aim to inflict a painful rebuke upon the Corinthians; instead, he desires to see them transformed so that the work of the gospel can go forward into other regions (2 Cor 10:15–16; compare 2 Cor 7:9–11). Paul desires to use the church at Corinth as a springboard to bring the gospel to the regions beyond them, likely to the west, such as Rome and Spain (compare Rom 15:28). Paul sees what many of us fail to see: that Jesus' work is about not just one individual, but the entire world. When one church is compromised and falls under the influence of Satan instead of Christ, it's not just the people in that community who take a hit; it's the work of the gospel everywhere. This is why it's so vital that each of us—not just as communities, but as individuals—aim to stay on track with Jesus.

## Making a Radical Commitment to Jesus

The overall Corinthian problem is rooted in listening to the wrong people and, as a consequence, failing to be accountable to Christ.

Believing in Jesus' ways requires radical commitment to transparency and accountability. In my life, I have seen this to be the true game-changer. I have a weekly accountability call with a close friend, and I rarely miss it. His only interest in my life is his desire to see me grow closer to Jesus. We don't work or do ministry together; we don't share many mutual friends—and that's intentional. We're not even regular donors to each other's ministries. Our success in life is mutually dependent, in the sense that we hold each other accountable to living fully for Jesus,

> Believing in Jesus' ways requires radical commitment to transparency and accountability.

but in no other way. As a result, my friend can tell me exactly like it is without any fear of repercussions and/or expectation of benefits. We trust each other with everything, from the most joyous moments of the week to the darkest thoughts that crossed our minds. Our goal is, as Paul says, to build each other up by "taking every thought captive to the obedience of Christ" (2 Cor 10:5). My decision to enter into this kind of accountability was one of the defining moments of my life, and our conversations are one of the most important events of my week. Our conversations help me follow Jesus more closely, give me accountability around my spiritual and life goals, and provide me with the opportunity to pray with someone about my struggles (both within myself and with others). These talks have been a significant way that I have cut ties with darkness in my life.

I believe that my friend and our relationship is the type of model we see in the Bible. The church is meant to serve as a way forward for us with our walk with Jesus. And our relationships that emerge from it should guide us to living for Jesus. One-on-one discipleship is one of the definitive ways that we will fall more in love with Jesus and live more fulfilling lives for him. We must cut ties with darkness together, pulling one another toward the realm of Christ.

As we center our lives on Christ, we can boast in his work in ourselves and in others; we can talk about how he has transformed us from within and done the miraculous (2 Cor 10:17). This is the only thing worth boasting about—people living according to the image of God through the saving work of Jesus.

As Paul tells us, we should never aim to commend ourselves, but instead let the Lord commend us (2 Cor 10:18; compare 11:1). So even when we speak about Jesus' work in us, the conversation should be about him, not us. The focus must always be the person of Christ, actively working to transform us and empower us to live according to God's image.

## How Lies Creep In

We can be led away from living in God's image by letting lies slowly creep in. As we begin to believe these lies, we lie to ourselves, and eventually we lie to others. We hide the truth about our spiritual walk and our failings. And this then leads to more lies.

Throughout 2 Corinthians, we see Paul affirming Jesus at work in the Corinthian community while being deeply aware that there are larger issues going on that are leading them away from Jesus. In 2 Corinthians 6:14–7:1, Paul shows the believers that they must withdraw from the people who have been influencing them to sin against him and against God. He finally tells them:

> For I am jealous for you with a godly jealousy, because I promised you in marriage to one husband, to present you as a pure virgin to Christ. But I am afraid lest somehow, as the serpent deceived Eve by his craftiness, your minds may be led astray from the sincerity and the purity of devotion to Christ. For if the one who comes proclaims another Jesus whom we have not proclaimed, or you receive a different spirit which you did not receive, or a different gospel which you did

not accept, you put up with it well enough!
(2 Cor 11:2–4).

Rather than being influenced by someone who can lead them to transformation—Paul—the Corinthian church is in danger of following people who will lead them toward Satan. Paul sarcastically calls these people "pre-eminent apostles" or "super-apostles," yet he is clear that he in no way considers himself inferior to them (2 Cor 11:5). And herein lies Paul's definition of heretics: those who preach a different gospel than he does.

## NOT-SO-SUPER APOSTLES

Paul's opponents in Corinth, the "super-apostles," spread lies concerning the gospel and about Paul himself. Unfortunately, false teachers were prominent throughout New Testament times (e.g., Acts 13:6–8; 2 Pet 2:1; and Paul's warning to Timothy in 1 Tim 1:20).

It's likely that these false apostles in Corinth downplayed Jesus' death on the cross and promoted his eloquence as a teacher instead. They probably were trying to portray Jesus more like a Greek philosopher than as the world's redeemer, who sacrifices himself for our sins.[3] In addition, the "gospel" of these false apostles likely dismissed the need for generosity, since Paul directly links generosity and the gospel a few paragraphs earlier (2 Cor 9:13). If the false apostles are part of the group that was essentially celebrating the man who was living in extreme sexual sin, then they were promoting a type of cheap grace and devaluing Jesus' sacrifice (1 Cor 5:1–2; compare 2 Cor 7:1).[4] This sort of pandering, combined with the false apostles' speaking abilities, had deceived the Corinthian church into a sort of "I'm OK, you're OK" type of theology, in which we're all saved and God just wants us to be happy.

The Corinthian problem is the same problem we face in many cultures today. People find pastors and churches that they self-identify with; they follow leaders who are often charismatic, who tell them only what they want to hear to ensure that people stay in the chairs of the church (compare 2 Cor 11:6). The job of teachers in the Church is not to tell us what we want to hear, but to be brutally honest with us, like Paul is. Our leaders should guide us toward Jesus—which will require that we change. And more often than not, change is painful.

**SUGGESTED READING**

☐ 2 Corinthians 10:1–11:6

☐ The book of Jude

## Reflection

Having read this chapter, are there any leaders you're currently looking up to that fit the profile of the "super-apostles" ("false apostles")? If so, what can you do to change this?

_____

_____

Do you have an accountability partner? If not, list some names of people who may be a good fit. If no one comes to mind, talk to your pastor about who could be a good fit.

_____

_____

_____

# SUPER-APOSTLES AND BOASTING IN JESUS

2 Corinthians 11:7–13:10

Paul was more than willing to endure hardship for the sake of the gospel. And it's with this in mind that Paul finally gets to the heart of the matter regarding the Corinthian believers' perception of him: They're failing to acknowledge how much he and others have given for their sake. Paul has shared the gospel freely with the Corinthians, at the cost of others—including the impoverished believers in Macedonia—even though Corinth was a rich community that likely had a wealthy church. And Paul says he will continue to give of himself freely—in part because he truly loves the Corinthians, but also in order to undermine the claims of the false apostles (2 Cor 11:7–12).

## For the Gospel's Sake

In juxtaposition to Paul, who operates for the gospel's sake, the super-apostles are "false apostles, deceitful workers, disguising themselves as apostles of Christ" (2 Cor 11:13). And Paul is not surprised at this because "Satan himself disguises himself as an angel of light" and, accordingly, "his servants also disguise themselves as servants of righteousness" (2 Cor 11:14–15). This is what Paul's worldview of Satan's realm versus Christ's realm is all about. This is what his command to separate from those who are part of Satan's realm comes down to: Those who operate under the assumption of a false gospel, whether by choice or by default, will ultimately deceive us. They will lead us astray. Being equally yoked is the precaution that prevents us from being guided by false "light," by Satan's ways.

Discerning between light and darkness is no easy matter. But we can know that, ultimately, God will issue judgment (justice): Paul tells us that the servants of Satan will have an "end ... according to their deeds" (2 Cor 11:15). We also can find discernment by looking at the kind of gospel that people proclaim: Does their gospel align with self-sacrifice for Jesus? Does it demonstrate generosity and show a life of purity (compare 7:1)? If it doesn't, then we can know they are leading us toward a "different gospel" that is not God's gospel—it's Satan's (2 Cor 11:4).

## Living According to the True Gospel

The whole incident with the Corinthians makes Paul frustrated—and perhaps even impatient. He is tired of watching the Corinthian believers be led astray by these false apostles, so he plays their game just a little, to make a point. He prefaces the boasting that he feels is necessary at this point by saying that what follows is not spoken with the Lord's authority, but instead is mere foolishness—boasting according to the flesh (2 Cor 11:16–21). The sarcasm is palpable.

Paul proceeds to note that he has the ultimate résumé for an apostle: He is Hebrew, an Israelite, a descendant of Abraham. He knows the heritage of the Christian faith, Judaism, and was raised in it. He also is a better servant of Christ than the false apostles (2 Cor 11:23). In addition, he has endured imprisonments, beatings, shipwrecks, and secret escapes; he has been hungry and thirsty and exposed to the elements; he has faced danger of all kinds and nearly died for the sake of Christ (2 Cor 11:24–27, 32–33). On top of all this, Paul has the daily anxiety of being concerned for all the churches (2 Cor 11:28). If there is anything worth boasting about for Christ, Paul has encountered it, and he knows that to honestly be the case. In his weakness, Paul shows people who Jesus is (2 Cor 11:29–31).

Paul's point: Who can give for the gospel what I have given? If there is anything worth boasting about, it's our weakness in Christ, who makes us strong (Phil 4:12–13). Christ can lead us and guide us in anything. Paul essentially is asking the super-apostles, "Are you more qualified in terms of heritage and learning than I? Are you more qualified in terms of the sacrifices you've made for Jesus?" The answer is absolutely not.

## Visions of the Beyond

Although Paul is fed up with the ridiculousness of having to defend himself before the Corinthians, he continues his argument by emphasizing spiritual experiences (2 Cor 12:1). To go on in his "boasting," to the shame of the Corinthian "super-apostles," Paul tells

the story of "a man in Christ" who was "caught up to
the third heaven"—this man may be him or someone
else (2 Cor 12:2–5).[1] Paul likely makes this point because of the heavy emphasis at Corinth on the spiritual (compare 1 Cor 11–13). If it is "spiritual" that the
Corinthians want, surely there are people more qualified than the "super-apostles." But even with this
clouded story—and with his remarks about wanting
people to believe only what they see and hear from
him and not trust him for any other reasons—Paul
is unafraid to hint at his own spiritual experiences
(2 Cor 12:6–7).

But Paul will not let the spiritual revelations be the
only guiding force here; he wants to emphasize for
the Corinthian believers that dependence on Christ is
to be much more valued:

> So that I would not exalt myself, a thorn in
> the flesh was given to me, a messenger of
> Satan, in order that it would torment me so
> that I would not exalt myself. Three times I
> appealed to the Lord about this, that it would
> depart from me. And he said to me, "My
> grace is sufficient for you, because the power
> is perfected in weakness." Therefore rather I
> will boast most gladly in my weaknesses, in
> order that the power of Christ may reside in
> me. Therefore I delight in weaknesses, in in-
> sults, in calamities, in persecutions and dif-
> ficulties for the sake of Christ, for whenever
> I am weak, then I am strong (2 Cor 12:7–10).[2]

Whatever the "thorn" is that Paul is experiencing,
and however it came about, his point remains clear:

Only God's grace can have any real lasting effects in Paul's life.[3] And only in our weakness, when we rely on Christ's strength, can we become the people we are meant to be.[4]

### WHAT IS THE "THORN"?

Although we can't know for sure what Paul meant by the "thorn in the flesh," probable suggestions include:

- his emotional struggles;
- his opponents;
- a physical disorder or deformity; and
- an evil force (in general or against him specifically).[5]

Paul's point also indicates that Satan clearly can oppose believers, causing evil and harm against them. By no means are Christians exempt from such oppression and persecution.[6] And although Satan may intend this opposition to cause harm, Christ can use it for good; and in Paul's case, Christ even allows for the "thorn" to go on so that Paul may continue to rely on him.

Paul understands that what people value is not what will save them; only Jesus can save. He also understands that difficulties might come our way that defy our comprehension. William Wilberforce, the great abolitionist who was afflicted with a severe disease for the majority of his life, once said:

> Let it not however surprise us ... [that there are] difficulties which we cannot fully comprehend. ... Scarcely is there an object

around us, that does not afford endless matter of doubt and argument. The meanest reptile which crawls on the earth ... every herb and flower which we behold, baffles ... our limited inquiries. All nature calls upon us to be humble. Can it then be surprising if we are at a loss on this question, which respects, not the properties of matter, or of numbers, but the counsels and ways of him whose "Understanding is infinite" (Psalm 147:5), "whose judgments are declared to be unsearchable, and his ways past finding out?" (Romans 11:33).[7]

God knows what we go through, and he knows the exact solution we need. We should always seek the miracle and always believe in it. And we should always believe that God desires to cast out the evil, ultimately. But we must also trust in how he acts, according to his timing. There are many things that we cannot possibly comprehend, that only God knows. Wilberforce understood this, and so did Paul. I have a friend who suffers regular spiritual and physical affliction, which he and others pray against often, but it continues to linger. And I believe that—like Paul, and perhaps like Wilberforce—God allows for this difficulty to go on to show my friend that Jesus' grace is sufficient.

> We should always seek the miracle and always believe in it. ... But we must also trust in how he acts, according to his timing.

It's this point that Paul so badly desires for the Corinthians to understand. Instead, they emphasize the strength of their "super-apostles" despite seeing the true signs—likely a reference to miracles—performed among them (2 Cor 12:11–12; compare 1 Cor 12:10). Out of some sort of ridiculous jealousy, and a clear lack of thankfulness—as well as the influence of false teachers—the Corinthian believers have allowed themselves to be led astray, away from the love and guidance of Paul (2 Cor 12:13). Paul will once again come to them, in the same spirit he did before—as one who will give of himself and not seek anything in return for his ministry—for the purpose of bringing them back in line with Jesus' ways. Paul acts this way because he is their spiritual parent (2 Cor 12:14–18).[8]

## The Change That Must Occur

Paul closes his very personal defense of his apostleship and ministry methods by emphasizing the point that he is not defending himself before the Corinthians, but rather is "speaking in Christ before God, and all these things … for [their] edification" (2 Cor 12:19). Paul is not the one in need of correction here; the Corinthians are. And in case we were wondering, "Just what is Paul concerned about?," he clarifies things for us: He is concerned that when he comes to the Corinthians, he will not find them as he wishes, living according to God's ways. Paul says, "I am afraid lest somehow when I arrive, I will not find you as I want, and I may be found by you as you do not want. I am afraid lest somehow there will be strife, jealousy, outbursts of anger, selfish ambition, slander, gossip, pride, disorder" (2 Cor 12:20).[9] Interestingly, Paul says he's also concerned that the Corinthians might not find *him* as *they* wish. He has emphasized that he does not feel inferior about his ministry, but some of them might still feel that way if they persist in focusing on outward appearances. Here, the problem lies not with Paul, but with the image that some believers want him to project. If they still believe a false gospel, they might hold misguided expectations for Paul that could become a source of conflict.

He also fears that when he arrives in Corinth he "will grieve over many of those who sinned previously and have not repented because of their impurity and sexual immorality and licentiousness that they have practiced" (2 Cor 12:21; compare 1 Cor 5:1–13). It is this darkness that may be looming over the church, and Paul knows that it will destroy them. For this reason, he mourns—which is exactly what ongoing sin should cause us to do. We are to separate from the darkness; we are to fight and flail against it in the power of the triumphant Christ (2 Cor 7:1).

## Getting to the Truth

In response to the identification of darkness, we should feel sadness and grief—and then embrace God's ways, which can overcome the darkness. We should emphasize the power of Christ to battle darkness and overtake it with his light. As part of that battle, it is our duty to lead others toward the light. But we must be cautious when bringing the truth to the light. The Corinthian believers were careless in their approach. They brought accusations against Paul (and likely against others) that were flat-out false, and when it came to condemning ongoing sin, they often failed to do so. To correct this, Paul offers the Corinthians a guideline that I believe that we should live by today: "By the testimony of two or three witnesses every word [or charge] will be established" (2 Cor 13:1; compare Deut 19:5; 17:6; compare Matt 18:16; 1 Tim 5:19). It is easy for someone to be falsely accused, so we discern by requiring multiple people to verify a charge.

But Paul does not just leave things at the point where witnesses must be established to verify any charges. He warns the Corinthians—as he did on his second visit (the "sorrowful visit")—that he will not tolerate falsehoods when he arrives (2 Cor 13:2–3).[10] Instead, he will confront those who must be corrected—the "super-apostles" and any who are continuing to practice abhorrent sins without repentance. Paul sees through the smoke and mirrors at Corinth; he knows that they believe that he is too meek to take bold actions. Nothing could be further from the truth. Paul emphasizes this point by circling back to Jesus, whom all this is really about:

> For indeed, [Jesus] was crucified because of weakness, but he lives because of the power of God. For we also are weak in him, but we will live together with him because of the power of God toward you. Test yourselves [then] to see if you are in the faith. Examine yourselves! Or do you not recognize regarding yourselves that Jesus Christ is in you, unless you are unqualified? (2 Cor 13:4–5).

This, then, is the measure for the Corinthians: Do they see Jesus reflected in their lives, or do they see merely their own image? And this should be the same question we ask ourselves: Do we find Jesus in us, or do we find ourselves? It is Jesus that connects Paul and the Corinthians—nothing more, nothing less. Jesus is sufficient!

Paul is unafraid to be tested before by the Corinthians—as his sarcasm in verse 6 shows— but he is decidedly prayerful about the situation with the Corinthians (2 Cor 13:6-7). Paul doesn't want to be right; he wants to see people living righteous lives for Jesus (2 Cor 13:7). As Christians, this must always be our desire. It's not about winning or losing; it's all about Jesus' victories. And if we're living for Jesus, we will be able to say what Paul can:

> Do they see Jesus reflected in their lives, or do they see merely their own image? … Do we find Jesus in us, or do we find ourselves?

> For we are not able to do anything against the truth, but rather only for the truth. For we rejoice whenever we are weak, but you are strong, and we pray for this: your maturity (2 Cor 13:8-9).

We should write and speak like Paul writes and speaks—for the purpose of seeing people come to Jesus, living fully committed lives, separated from the darkness and united to the living and resurrected one (2 Cor 13:10). And when God grants us authority to do his work, we should use it for the purposes of his glory and his glory alone!

> **SUGGESTED READING**
>
> ☐   2 Corinthians 11:7–13:10
>
> ☐   Romans 11:13–12:2

## Reflection

Examine closely the list of sins that Paul worries he will find at Corinth (2 Cor 12:20–21). Which of these sins are you practicing or struggling to avoid? Bring these sins to the light so that you can find freedom from them. Who can you confess your sins to? What action do you plan to take to cut off your ties with darkness?

_____

_____

What expectations that are actually ungodly do you currently have of Christian leaders? How can you change these?

_____

_____

_____

What expectations do you have of yourself that are ungodly? How can you change these? What can you do to center your life on Christ and cut ties with darkness?

_____

_____

# CONCLUSION

At the end of *The Return of the King*, Frodo says, "My dear Sam, you cannot always be torn in two. You will have to be one and whole for many years. You have so much to enjoy and to be and to do. Your part in the story will go on."[1] Frodo knows that life will never be the same after the past pain of bearing the ring but that life can be rebuilt for those who are ready to do so. His friend Sam must start his life anew in the Shire, centered on beauty and truth, in the beautiful green grass of creation.

Likewise, the Corinthians must live a new life centered on Christ—there is so much of their story yet to be told, and Paul wants it to be told as part of God's grand narrative.

And I know how beautiful this narrative is because I have seen it with my own eyes. I see the beauty and truth and hope in my wife's ocean-blue eyes now—something I could have never seen all those years ago in depression and misery. This is my daily rainbow, my reminder of God's providence.

I see my ministry life not just restored, but strong in the freedom of Christ—with the liberty to decide what is best for the ministry, in terms of both building relationships and dismissing others. Likewise, I can decide the same for my personal life—what relationships are only causing harm, and which ones are building me up? How can I lead people to Jesus—change the world—instead of becoming like them and the world?

I have freedom from the lions and hyenas, and I get to enjoy life with the zebras and gazelles. I get to live a life of discernment with the power of Christian friends around me—examining the gray to determine what is God's will and what is not. And I now rarely have doubts about when it's time to cut ties with people who will only represent darkness, because I pray and ask others for godly advice. As a result, my life is much healthier; I can now see God's work reflected in the world in street markets and cities, in the people he made and their creations.

And I see the liberty of life lived for Jesus in accountability. I have freedom from the sins that used to plague me and regularly work to overcome others that surface in my life. In transparency, darkness has little room to hide.

> In transparency, darkness has little room to hide.

I have so much further to go, but I look forward to God's story not just interweaving with mine, but overwhelming it—taking hold of it. I look forward to more of life being centered on Christ—not torn in two, between darkness and Jesus, but whole in Christ's resurrected life.

We are called to center our lives on Jesus, care for the impoverished, and bring the gospel to the ends of the earth. And everything we do, and every entanglement with darkness, can affect this work. As we center ourselves on Christ, it is not just our lives that improve; our *entire world* improves.

Paul shows us an example of fearless love in 2 Corinthians. He teaches us what it means to cut ties with darkness and center ourselves on Christ. He also shows us the beauty of doing so.

Paul indicates that, on this third visit of his to Corinth, he will not be afraid to call the believers into accountability, even though his previous visits had been painful (2 Cor 2:1; 12:20–21; 13:1). Paul knows that it is time for the Corinthians to get over their arrogance and their love of the "super-apostles," who simply tell them what they want to hear, and instead start following the ways of Jesus again. Sadly, the Corinthians' lives are currently aligning more with Satan's realm than with Christ's; this must change (2 Cor 6:15). And if Paul doesn't tell them, who will?

Paul is the church-planter who brought the Corinthians to Christ, after all, so if anyone is allowed to say "sorrowful" words to them, it's him (2 Cor 10:14; 11:5). Paul hopes that, from his letter, the Corinthian believers will not only learn to respect him again, and to live lives of purity, but that they will also join him in bringing the gospel to the ends of the earth and in supporting other believers who are in need (2 Cor 8:9–15; 9:1–7; 10:13–18). Paul understands that it is not only their lives that hang in the balance but also the lives of others.

Paul has overextended himself for the Corinthians. But even so, if he must boast to them—to defend his ministry as the ignorant "super-apostles" do— he will boast in his weakness, for this is what truly shows who Jesus is (2 Cor 12:5-6, 10; 12:8). Paul will do what he must to get the church to respond according to the way that Christians should (2 Cor 13:4-5). The Corinthians shouldn't be disputing with Paul; instead, they should be joining him in caring for the impoverished and in bringing the gospel to those who have yet to hear Jesus' name.

To inspire you to center your life fully on Jesus and to cut ties with darkness, I leave you with a paraphrase of Paul's closing words (2 Cor 13:11–14):

> Finally, brothers and sisters, rejoice! Be restored and be encouraged. And be in agreement about your decision to be centered on Jesus! Be at peace! And may the God of love and peace will be with you.
>
> Greet one another with kindness and in the spirit of reconciliation.
>
> All the believers in Jesus, made holy by him, greet you.
>
> May the grace of the Lord Jesus Christ and the love of God, and the fellowship of the Holy Spirit, be with all of you!

# FLESH AND LAW IN PAUL'S THEOLOGY

Living as people of God is a challenge—one that weighs heavily on the true Christian. We have an opportunity to rise with Christ or to continue falling into ways of sin. One of the greatest difficulties for the Christian is navigating this path. These challenges are at the front of Paul's mind in 2 Corinthians.

## Being Human While Despising Sin

Paul despises sin, and he uses the word "flesh" nearly synonymously with "sin." He says, "For when we were in the flesh, sinful desires were working through the law in our members, to bear fruit for death," and, "For I know that good does not live in me, that is, in my flesh. For the willing is present in me, but the doing of the good is not" (Rom 7:14, 18). This presents us with an apparent dilemma: How can we be human, in the flesh, yet hate our flesh?

Are we to desire only spiritual things and set aside everything of the flesh? Are we to mutilate our bodies to become more spiritual like some monks of old?

Should we stop caring and just eat poorly? Can we just do what we want with our bodies (as it appears some Corinthians were doing) because our spirit is already saved? Is that what Paul means when he contrasts the flesh and the spirit?

None of these ideas corresponds with Paul's worldview. In 1 Corinthians, Paul asks, "Do you not know that your body is the temple of the Holy Spirit who is in you, whom you have from God, and you are not your own?" (1 Cor 6:19). Or, as Paul puts it in 2 Corinthians 6:16, "[W]hat agreement [has the] temple of God with idols? For we are a temple of [the] living God. Just as God said, 'I will dwell in them and walk among [them], and I will be their God and they will be my people.' "[1]

For Paul, we are the very temple of God—us, in our bodies. Paul does not despise being human; he despises the corrupt nature that has crept into humanity. The flesh is not inherently evil, but the desires that we humans have are often evil. God loves his creation—which is us (including our bodies)—and he is using every part of us to overcome the evil that exists in his creation. As scholar Steven E. Runge puts it:

> Jesus' death and resurrection not only conquered death once and for all, it enabled believers to have new life as well (Rom 6:4; Col 3:1-3). Paul describes a twofold division between the flesh and the spirit. The flesh refers to God's originally perfect creation, which is now mortal and in decay as result of sin entering the world through Adam (Rom 5:12). The spirit is the essence of who we are, the part of us that lives on after our physical bodies die. In 2 Corinthians 4:16,

> Paul contrasts the two, stating that our outer person is being destroyed as our inner one is being renewed.[2]

For Paul, the spirit can override the flesh; this is how we find spiritual resurrection now (1 Cor 15:44). This is how we are transformed by the renewing of our minds, as he says elsewhere (Rom 12:2). This is why the Corinthians shouldn't knowingly eat meat sacrificed to idols and why they should abstain from sexual immorality (1 Cor 8:10–13; 6:13). This idea is what sets up Paul's language in 2 Corinthians 6:14: "Do not be unequally yoked." Paul is not just talking about the problem of a Christian marrying a non-Christian (as so many make this verse about, even though the topic of marriage is never raised in 2 Corinthians); he is talking about each and every relationship that is influential on your practices and values (including your marriage).

If God is redeeming our corrupt flesh and remaking it into his image, then we must make the tough decisions to collaborate with him in that process (2 Cor 4:4). We cannot allow for the most vital parts of our lives to be under the influence of those who accept less of their lives, who have not chosen to collaborate with God. This means family relationships, business partnerships, and influential friendships. And Paul is not just talking about Christians versus non-Christians here; he also is talking about the

> If God is redeeming our corrupt flesh and remaking it into his image, then we must make the tough decisions to collaborate with him in that process.

levels of discipleship. The Corinthian context, with so many problems going on in the church itself, shows that there are clear levels of spiritual maturity and commitment. Paul expects us to be equally yoked in terms of commitment level, too.

This comes to the forefront when Paul brings up the man who was in an incestuous relationship. He tells the Corinthian community to "hand over such a person to Satan for the destruction of the flesh, in order that his spirit may be saved in the day of the Lord" (1 Cor 5:5). In using this phrasing, Paul indicates that someone who is perpetually committing evil and then expelled from the church *can* ultimately come to repentance. This repentance is representative of the spirit transforming the flesh, leading to their very salvation.[3]

The gospel is not permission to go on sinning—or permission to deny being human. The gospel is the redemption of our entire selves. We are "a new creation" in Christ (2 Cor 5:17). Jesus did not die so that we could go on sinning, but so that we might be able to overcome sin. Jesus died so that everything might be saved. Jesus wants *all* of you to be transformed, not just part of you. As Jesus transforms us, we learn to live in God's image.

Bearing God's image is precisely what Jesus did. He was fully human and fully God—showing what it means to really be a person. In taking on human flesh, Jesus showed that flesh is not evil, but what we do with it can be. Paul goes so far as to say that "our struggle is not against blood and flesh, but against the rulers, against the authorities, against the world rulers of this darkness, against the spiritual forces of wickedness" (Eph 6:12). In another place, Paul talks about the difficulties of fighting against sin: "For I know that good does not live in me, that is, in my flesh. For the willing is present in me, but the doing of the good is not" (Rom 7:18). It is not bad to be human or to have a physical body; it's bad to live according to our selfish desires—which Paul metaphorically calls "the flesh."

To overcome these difficulties, we need to have the most influential people in our lives be at the same or a slightly higher spiritual-maturity level than we are. We need to see in their flesh the ability to live according to the Spirit. We need to see them working toward loving God with everything they have, and as a consequence loving their neighbor as themselves (Matt 22:39; Mark 12:31). This is the true mark of a Christian (1 John 2:3, 15; 3:10).

## Love and the Law

Much of 2 Corinthians is Paul addressing the debate of how we live according to God's will while still being human. Right in line with this debate are Paul's remarks about the Jewish law.[4] His critique and thoughts on this topic are severe; they are a message for those of us today who attempt to live simply according to prescriptions of the Bible rather than the guidance of the Spirit. They also provide guidance for we who attempt to make Christianity simply a set of regulations. Jesus wants more for us and desires more.

Paul contrasts the spirit with the flesh, while also contrasting God's Spirit with the law (2 Cor 3:7–18; compare Gal 3:2). Paul refers to "the ministry of death in letters carved on stone" and says that it is "transitory," like the glory that shone on Moses' face when he received the law (2 Cor 3:7). But God does not desire simple transitory glory for us; he desires for us to live: "For if what was transitory came with glory, by much more what remains is with glory" (2 Cor 3:11). We are then to live as people who practice "the ministry of righteousness [that] overflow[s] with glory" (2 Cor 3:9).

We live today in the freedom of God, "being transformed into the same image [his image] from glory into glory, just as from the Lord, the Spirit" (2 Cor 3:17–18). This is God's desire for our lives.

It is not that the law ever saved anyone. As Nijay K. Gupta puts it, "The Torah is like [a] spare tire."[5] The law handles things for the time being, but it's not a long-term solution. In addition, we can blow out a tire and not know how to use the spare, rendering it useless. The law in and of itself was not able to handle our problems; it was only the appropriate use of the law that sustained Israel for a time. Similarly, the work of the Holy Spirit can handle our problems today, but if we ignore it, we render it useless, too. We end up living purely according to the flesh, when we have access to a much greater power that could work within us.

> The law handles things for the time being, but it's not a long-term solution.

And this is why it's so dangerous when we allow the primary influences in our lives to be people who live according to "the flesh" or simply according to the law, which is capable of much less than God's Spirit. These people will convince us that we can handle things on our own, without the power of God at work in our lives. They will tell us things that seem right according to the flesh, according to ways of our culture; that approach will only lead us down the wrong path. God's ways are not our ways.

# PAUL AND THE "THIRD HEAVEN"

John D. Barry and Miles Custis

In 2 Corinthians 12:1–2, Paul describes how he was "caught up to the third heaven" (2 Cor 12:2). Two verses later, he adds that he was "caught up to paradise" (2 Cor 12:4). Paul could be indicating that there are three levels of heaven, with the "third heaven" and "paradise" being synonymous. If so, Paul's repetition of the phrase usually translated as "in the body or apart from the body" (2 Cor 12:2) is parallelism comparable to Hebrew poetry. Alternatively, he could be indicating that "paradise" is higher than the "third heaven." Paul could be moving through the heavens—into the third heaven in 2 Cor 12:3 and into a higher heaven in 2 Cor 12:4.

According to ancient cosmology, there are seven levels: the sky, the clouds, the sky above the clouds, the firmament, the waters above the firmament, the heavens, and the heaven of heavens, where God dwells. The three heavens view understands the first heaven to be the visible sky or the "firmament" (see

Gen 1:8 and note), the second heaven to either be the "heavens" or the division between the "heavens" (the "waters above the firmament"; Psa 148:4), and the third to be the "heavens of heavens" or "highest heavens" (1 Kgs 8:27; Psa 148:4). All views agree on the places, but they label them differently.

Paul is probably drawing from a background of Jewish pseudepigraphical literature written a few hundred years prior to him. Many of these postexilic writings describe individuals having visions of or making journeys to heaven. They typically portray heaven as having several levels or different heavens.

Many of these writings portray up to seven different levels of heaven (see 2 *Enoch* 21:2). If Paul is drawing from these sources, he could be indicating that "paradise" is higher than the "third heaven." Other writings portray only three levels of heaven. The *Apocalypse of Moses*, for example, links the two together as it portrays the archangel Michael taking Adam's body to "paradise" or the "third heaven" where he will wait for his future resurrection (*Apocalypse of Moses* 37:5). Based on these texts, it is possible that Paul is using the "third heaven" and "paradise" interchangeably.

Another writing that portrays three levels of heaven is the *Testament of Levi*. Paul may have been drawing specifically from this resource. In it, Levi enters heaven in a dream (*Testament of Levi* 2:5-12). He describes three heavens, the third of which is for the "holy ones" (*Testament of Levi* 3:1-3). The second heaven is the location of God's armies who are waiting to judge "Belial." Paul may have also been drawing from the *Testament of Levi* in 2 Cor 6:14-15 when he contrasts Belial with Christ (as well as light with darkness). *Testament of Levi*

19:1 states, "Choose for yourselves light or darkness, the Law of the Lord or the works of Belial."

Most likely, Paul is describing an experience where he was brought up to the presence of God. As *Testament of Levi* states, "In the uppermost heaven of all dwells the Great Glory in the Holy of Holies superior to all holiness" (*Testament of Levi* 3:3). Paul cites this "vision" and "revelation" (2 Cor 12:1) to show his authority and emphasize his ministry as divinely appointed. Even though this experience was "extraordinary," Paul does not use it to boast or exalt himself (2 Cor 12:6–7).[1]

## Labeling the Ancient Cosmology of the Universe

| Ancient Cosmology | Seven Heavens Labeling | Three Heavens Labeling | Alternative Three Heavens Labeling |
| --- | --- | --- | --- |
| The heaven of heavens | Seventh heaven | Third heaven (paradise) | Paradise |
| The heavens | Sixth heaven | Second heaven | Third heaven |
| The waters above the firmament | Fifth heaven | | Second heaven |
| The firmament | Fourth heaven | First heaven | First heaven |
| Above the clouds | Third heaven | | |
| The clouds | Second heaven | | |
| The skies | First heaven | | |

# BIBLIOGRAPHY OF ACADEMIC WORKS

## Exegetical Tools

Aune, David E. "Digression." Pages 132–33 in *The Westminster Dictionary of the New Testament and Early Christian Literature and Rhetoric*. By David E. Aune. Louisville, KY: Westminster John Knox, 2003.

Barry, John D., Michael S. Heiser, Miles C. Custis, Douglas Mangum, Matthew M. Whitehead, and Michael R. Grigoni, eds. *Faithlife Study Bible*. Bellingham, WA: Lexham Press, 2012.

Barry, John D., Lazarus Wentz, Douglas Mangum, Carrie Sinclair-Wolcott, Rachel Klippenstein, David Bomar, Elliot Ritzema, Wendy Widder, and Derek R. Brown, eds. *The Lexham Bible Dictionary*. Bellingham, WA: Lexham Press, 2012–2014.

Betz, Hans Dieter. "Corinthians, The Second Epistle to The." Pages 1148–53 in vol. 1 of *The Anchor Bible Dictionary*. Edited by David Noel Freedman. New York: Doubleday, 1996.

Brown, Derek R., and E. Tod Twist. *Lexham Bible Guide: 1 Corinthians*. Edited by John D. Barry and Douglas Mangum. Bellingham, WA: Lexham Press, 2013.

Brown, Derek R., Wendy Widder, and E. Tod Twist. *Lexham Bible Guide: 2 Corinthians*. Edited by John D. Barry and Douglas Mangum. Bellingham, WA: Lexham Press, 2013.

Garland, David E. *2 Corinthians*. New American Commentary 29. Nashville: Broadman & Holman, 1999.

Harris, Murray J. *The Second Epistle to the Corinthians: A Commentary on the Greek Text*. New International Greek Testament Commentary. Grand Rapids: Eerdmans, 2005

O'Connor, J. Murphy. "Corinth." Pages 1134–39 in vol. 1 of *The Anchor Bible Dictionary*. Edited by David Noel Freedman. New York: Doubleday, 1996.

Metzger, Bruce M. *A Textual Commentary on the Greek New Testament*. 2nd ed. Stuttgart: Deutsche Bibelgesellschaft, 1994.

# Secondary Sources

Aland, Barbara, and Kurt Aland. *The Text of the New Testament: An Introduction to the Critical Editions and to the Theory and Practice of Modern Textual Criticism*. Translated by Erroll F. Rhodes. 2nd ed. Grand Rapids: Eerdmans, 1995.

Barry, John D. "Early Evidence of Subjective Interpretation in the Subjective Interpretation in the Pesharim of Qumran." *Revue Scriptura*, new series 9 (2007): 119–38.

Beale, G. K. "The Old Testament Background of Reconciliation in 2 Corinthians 5-7 and Its Bearing on the Literary Problems of 2 Corinthians 6:14-7:1." *New Testament Studies* 35 (1989): 550–81.

Betz, Hans Dieter. "2 Cor 6:14-7:1: An Anti-Pauline Fragment?" *Journal of Biblical Literature* 92, no. 1 (March 1973): 88–108.

Brown, Derek R. *"The God of This Age": Satan in the Churches and Letters of the Apostle Paul*. Wissenschaftliche Untersuchungen zum Neuen Testament II. Tübingen: Mohr Siebeck, forthcoming.

Childs, Brevard S. *Biblical Theology in Crisis*. Philadelphia: Westminster, 1970.

———. *The Church's Guide for Reading Paul*. Grand Rapids: Eerdmans, 2008.

———. *The New Testament as Canon*. New York: Continuum, 1992.

Fitzmyer, Joseph A. "Qumran and the Interpolated Paragraph in 2 Corinthians 6:14-7:1." *Catholic Biblical Quarterly* 23, no. 3 (July 1961): 271–80.

Martin, Ralph P. *2 Corinthians*. Word Biblical Commentary 40. Waco, TX: Word, 1986.

Steudel, Annette. "God and Belial." Pages 332–40 in *The Dead Sea Scrolls Fifty Years after their Discovery: Proceedings of the Jerusalem Congress, July 20-25, 1997*. Edited by Lawrence H. Schiffman, Emanuel Tov, James C. VanderKam, and Galen Marquis. Jerusalem: Israel Museum, 2000.

Witherington, Ben III. *Conflict and Community in Corinth: A Socio-Rhetorical Commentary on 1 and 2 Corinthians*. Grand Rapids: Eerdmans, 1995.

Wise, Michael, Martin Abegg Jr., and Edward Cook. *The Dead Sea Scrolls: A New Translation*. New York: HarperCollins, 2005.

# BIBLIOGRAPHY OF
# OTHER SOURCES

Anderson, Neil T. *The Bondage Breaker*. Eugene, OR: Harvest House, 2006.

Barry, John D. *The Resurrected Servant in Isaiah*. Downers Grove, IL: InterVarsity Press, 2010.

Barry, John D., and Miles Custis. *2 Peter & Jude: Contend for the Faith*. Not Your Average Bible Study Series. Bellingham, WA: Lexham Press, 2014.

Barry, John D., Jake Mailhot, David Bomar, Elliot Ritzema, and Carrie Sinclair-Wolcott, eds. *DIY Bible Study*. Bellingham, WA: Lexham Press, 2014.

Bartholomew, Craig G. *When You Want to Yell at God: The Book of Job*. Bellingham, WA: Lexham Press, 2014.

Bartholomew, Craig G., and Michael W. Goheen. *The True Story of the Whole World*. Grand Rapids: Faith Alive Christian Resources, 2004.

Bunyan, John. *Pilgrim's Progress*. 1678. Repr., London: James Clarke, 1987.

Corbett, Steve, and Brian Fikkert. *When Helping Hurts*. Chicago: Moody, 2009.

Custis, Miles, and John D. Barry. "Paul and the 'Third Heaven.'" *Faithlife Study Bible*. Edited by John D. Barry. Bellingham, WA: Lexham Press, 2012.

Gupta, Nijay K. "The Torah: Like a Spare Tire." *Bible Study Magazine*, September/October 2010, 31.

Heiser, Michael S. "Who is the God of this World?" *Bible Study Magazine*, January/February 2014, 44–45.

Kuyper, Abraham. "Sphere Sovereignty." Pages 461–90 in *Abraham Kuyper: A Centennial Reader*. Edited by James D. Bratt. Grand Rapids: Eerdmans, 1998.

Lupton, Robert. *Toxic Charity*. San Francisco: HarperCollins, 2012.

Manning, Brennan. *Ruthless Trust*. Grand Rapids: Zondervan, 2009.

Markham, Beryl. *West with the Night*. Boston: Houghton Mifflin, 1942. Repr., New York: Farrar, Straus & Giroux, 2013.

Miller, Donald. *Searching for God Knows What*. Nashville: Thomas Nelson, 2004.

Peters, Randall Mark, Dave Phillips, and Quentin Steen. *Colors of God*. Downers Grove, IL: InterVarsity Press, 2010.

Runge, Steven E. "Spirit and Flesh in Paul's Letters." *Faithlife Study Bible*. Edited by John D. Barry. Bellingham, WA: Lexham Press, 2012.

Swindoll, Charles R. *Job: A Man of Heroic Endurance*. Nashville: Thomas Nelson, 2004.

Wilberforce, William. *A Practical View of Christianity*. 1797. Repr., Peabody, MA: Hendrickson, 1996.

# NOTES

## Chapter 1. Introduction: The Threads of Life

1. *The Lord of the Rings: The Return of the King*, directed by Peter Jackson (Los Angeles: New Line Cinema, 2003).

2. Throughout 2 Corinthians, Paul shows that he may appear "weak" to the Corinthian church, but his weakness is actually strength in Christ. Paul is "weak" only in the way that God deems appropriate, which is complete dependence on him (e.g., 2 Cor 6:3–13; 11:30; 12:5, 9–10; 13:4).

3. Acts first records that Paul stayed "a year and six months" in Corinth. During this time, he was working as a tentmaker with Priscilla and Aquila (a husband-and-wife ministry team; Acts 18:2–3, 11). Acts then records that Paul stayed longer at Corinth, leading to much controversy and eventually a trial before the proconsul Gallio (Acts 18:12–17). This additional period of time is unknown in length. Timothy and Silas are with him during the majority of his time at Corinth; they came down from Macedonia (Acts 18:5).

4. The theory that the Corinthians sent Paul a letter full of questions is based primarily on the question and answer format of 1 Corinthians and the fact that it seems unlikely that he would have left Corinth before addressing such practical questions if he would have known that they were open issues at the time.

5. After writing 1 Corinthians, it seems likely that Paul sent Timothy to Corinth, based on his comment in 1 Cor 16:10–11. Paul specifically notes that he will visit the Corinthian church after traveling through Macedonia, after his time in Ephesus (1 Cor 16:5), but Acts never records his "sorrowful visit" after his time in Ephesus.

6. Paul's language in 1 Cor 5:13 and 2 Cor 6:14–7:1 picks up on a refrain from the Old Testament (Deut 13:5; 17:7, 12; 21:21; 22:21–22, 24; Judg 20:13).

7. Paul's "sorrowful letter" could have been incorporated into the letter we know as 2 Corinthians or be a reference to

1 Corinthians, but it's likely another letter that has not been preserved. This makes the letter we know as 2 Corinthians Paul's fourth letter to the Corinthian Christians. (It's also possible that Paul's remark in 2 Cor 7:6–13 is a reference to an additional letter, not the same "sorrowful letter." If this is the case, then 2 Corinthians is actually Paul's fifth letter—with two "sorrowful letters" coming before it, neither of which have been preserved.)

The viewpoint presented here, that Paul's "sorrowful letter" is no longer preserved (and, likewise, that the letter he penned prior to 1 Corinthians is no longer preserved), relies on the view that these letters were not incorporated into 1 and 2 Corinthians. However, it remains possible that they *were* incorporated into 1 and 2 Corinthians.

One possible explanation for the various parts of 2 Corinthians is that it is actually a sequence of multiple letters that were later assembled as one letter; another view is that Paul wrote over three to nine months. The basics of this theory and the debate surrounding it is explained in Derek R. Brown, Wendy Widder, and E. Tod Twist, *Lexham Bible Guide: 2 Corinthians*, ed. John D. Barry and Douglas Mangum (Bellingham, WA: Lexham Press, 2013). The focus of the debate is 2 Cor 10–13, which could be related to a different historical situation than the rest of the book (or even be Paul's "sorrowful letter"). The precise dating of 2 Corinthians, or its various parts, also is wrapped up in this debate. However, it seems reasonable to conclude that Paul wrote the various components of 2 Corinthians sometime in AD 56 during his third missionary journey, with the majority of it penned in Macedonia (modern-day northern Greece).

Second Corinthians 6:14–7:1 is the only section of the letter for which Paul's authorship is disputed. In contrast to this view, my treatment of 2 Cor 6:14–7:1 in this book shows its connection to the rest of the letter. Regardless of whether we think this passage is authentically written by Paul, I think that we as Christians must wrestle with it because it is part of the canonical 2 Corinthians. Furthermore, even if I were to concede that 2 Cor 6:14–7:1 was not authentically Paul's, I would still have to wrestle with the question of why an editor—sometime prior to the canonization of the Bible and all early manuscripts—decided that it was worth inserting at this point in the letter.

Ultimately, I interpret 2 Corinthians (and all biblical books for that matter) in their canonical form, for the basic reasons stated above. In the introduction of my book *The Resurrected Servant in Isaiah* (Downers Grove, IL: InterVarsity Press, 2010), I further discuss my view. Brevard S. Childs is the scholar whose work most influenced my interpretive lens on this matter. See Brevard S. Childs, Biblical *Theology in Crisis* (Philadelphia: Westminster, 1970); *The New Testament as Canon* (New York: Continuum, 1992); *The Church's Guide for Reading Paul* (Grand Rapids: Eerdmans, 2008).

8. It could even be argued that, for Paul, his relationship with the Corinthians goes beyond mere responsibility; he is obligated before God to see that they follow Jesus. It's a calling much like fatherhood (2 Cor 12:14–15).

9. The Corinthian church seems fragmented—and at least when Paul wrote 1 Corinthians, they certainly were (1 Cor 1:10–16). Paul's remarks in 2 Corinthians apply to the whole church in the sense that all of them should live his commandments, live according to his example, and embrace him as their leader. But it seems highly likely that some of the Corinthian believers were already on track, and thus Paul's message was really affirming what they already knew.

When I speak of Corinthian believers in this book, I'm focusing on those who need Paul's rebuke (unless I specify otherwise). I also identify a subset of this group, "the false apostles" about whom Paul has a particular message.

10. To understand what I mean by this comment—i.e., my interpretation of Paul on this matter—see "What the Gospel Requires" and "The Struggle of Being Human" in chapter 6.

11. This outline is adapted from Derek R. Brown, Wendy Widder, and E. Tod Twist, *Lexham Bible Guide: 2 Corinthians*, ed. John D. Barry and Douglas Mangum (Bellingham, WA: Lexham Press, 2013).

12. My own translation.

13. At one point I edited a book on this topic, which is the likely inception of this idea in my mind: Randall Mark Peters, Dave Phillips, and Quentin Steen, *Colors of God* (Downers Grove, IL: InterVarsity Press, 2010). I don't necessarily agree with the details of the authors' discussion in this work, but I do like the

overall concept of a God who has a colorful personality; it is this same idea that I will employ in this book.

14. See my later discussion regarding Paul's use of the law in chapter 2, "The Tough Decisions Christians Must Make."

15. The idea of offering a better narrative with your life has been brought up by many Christian thinkers. The most influential on me personally are Donald Miller, Craig G. Bartholomew, and Michael Goheen; see Donald Miller, *Searching for God Knows What* (Nashville: Thomas Nelson, 2004); Craig G. Bartholomew and Michael W. Goheen, *The True Story of the Whole World* (Grand Rapids: Faith Alive Christian Resources, 2004).

## Chapter 2. The Tough Decisions Christians Must Make

1. Some textual witnesses read here, "For you (plural) are a temple of [the] living God" (underlined words represent variants in the different textual witnesses). Other witnesses read, "For we are temples of [the] living God." One church father reads, "Therefore we are temples of the living God" once, and another time "That we may be temples of God." "For we are a temple of [the] living God" is the most likely *Urtext*, based upon external and internal evidence, as well as the immediate and broader literary context of 2 Corinthians. (Translations contained in this note are my own.)

The other textual variants in 2 Cor 6:14–7:1 will not be discussed in detail, since they are either poorly attested by the textual witnesses or they are based on grammatical or orthographical preference.

2. Some argue that the use of flesh and spirit together in 7:1c is not Pauline in character, since Paul usually contrasts the two (e.g., Rom 8:4–13). Ralph P. Martin, *2 Corinthians*, Word Biblical Commentary 40 (Waco, TX: Word, 1986), 208–10, argues that since Paul usually contrasts the "flesh" and "spirit" and the "cleansing of flesh and spirit" "smacks of a Qumranite theology" (e.g., 1QS 3:8), this verse, along with the whole passage, is an interpolation of a Qumran fragment. Although 7:1 does have some Qumranite theological elements, one cannot assume from a few parallels that the passage was drawn from Qumranite literature. Martin has completely ignored 5:10, which clarifies Paul's usage of his metaphor here. It is not beyond Paul to use the "flesh and spirit" metaphor in multiple

ways. In Paul's other usages he has drawn on the metaphor to describe the difference between the way one lives that is inspired by the Spirit and the way one acts who is controlled by the flesh (e.g., Rom 8:4–13). In 2 Cor 7:1a, Paul is using the metaphor to talk about one's accountability for his or her actions before Christ—actions that are done both by flesh and by the spirit (i.e., outwardly and inwardly). Paul is using two separate metaphors that cannot be equated. Even if one does wish to argue they are the same metaphor, it is not beyond Paul to progress in his theology and begin to understand something he previously did not understand. It is also not beyond him to appropriate theological elements from the *ethos*, whether it be from Qumran or from somewhere else, to explain his argument. David E. Garland, *2 Corinthians*, New American Commentary 29 (Nashville: Broadman & Holman Publishers, 1999), 341–43, draws similar conclusions to the ones I have drawn when he states that "purifying themselves and perfecting their holiness would mean, in this context, withdrawing from any unholy alliances and association with idolatry."

Paul usually defines what is mortal with the word "flesh" (e.g., Rom 8:5–6). Paul's language concerning "what is mortal being swallowed up by life" suggests that Paul understood the flesh to be subordinate to the spirit but yet something that still must be dealt with (2 Cor 5:4–5). Furthermore, in 2 Cor 5:10 Paul states that each person will receive "what is due for what he has done in the body, whether good or evil" when they "appear before the judgment seat of Christ." This verse suggests that Paul understood the necessity to do what was right in the flesh, and therefore he would have no qualm with suggesting that believers cleanse themselves from defilement in the "flesh and spirit" (i.e., in their outward and inward parts). For more on Paul's use of the term "flesh," see the appendix, "Flesh and Law in Paul's Theology." (Translations in this note are my own.)

3. My own translation.

4. Paul's opening to 2 Cor 7:1 is a hortatory subjunctive, so although it's not technically an imperative, it functions like one—paralleling the imperative in 2 Cor 6:14 that opened the section.

5. "Ourselves" in 2 Cor 1 implies that both the community and the individual is in view.

Since the term *molysmou* is a *hapax legomenon* in the New Testament, occurring only in 2 Cor 7:1, it is very difficult to define—forcing us to look at its use within its semantic domain in the New Testament and then beyond the New Testament for further insights. When we conduct this study, we see that the term *molysmou* (μολυσμοῦ) is best understood and translated as "defilement" in 2 Cor 7:1. It is primarily (though not always) a religious term, which has to do with inward (spirit) and outward (flesh) defilement of the person (e.g., Strabo, *Geographica*, 17.2.4; Jer 23:15 LXX; Titus 1:15; Rev 3:4). The term can also mean "wound." The primary kind of "defilement" in relation to 2 Cor 7:1 was likely caused by cultic idol worshiping in thought or action (e.g., 1 Cor 8:7; 2 Cor 6:16).

The term *molysmou* is primarily used in 2 Cor 7:1 to make the Corinthian community aware of the separation from God (and possibly the community of God) that will occur if they are "unequally yoked" with "unbelievers." Since the "unbelievers" have a keen association with idols, there is no doubt that their influence can "defile" the "believers", both in "flesh" (outwardly) and "spirit" (inwardly).

6. For more on this topic, see the appendix, "Flesh and Law in Paul's Theology."

7. See "The Reign of Jesus and the Fight against Beliar," later in this chapter.

8. The rhetorical digression in 2 Cor 6:14–7:1 is demarcated by the *Wiederaufnahme* technique in 6:13 and 7:2. A digression can be defined as an "insertion of a relatively long and independent segment into a text with which it is somehow thematically connected." See David E. Aune, "Digression," *The Westminster Dictionary of New Testament and Early Christian Literature and Rhetoric* (Louisville, KY: Westminster John Knox, 2003), 132–33.

Second Corinthians 6:14–7:1 is identified here as a digression, rather than an interpolation, because of the repetitive *inclusio* in 6:13 and 7:2. Second Corinthians 6:13 ends with the phrase "also open wide for us," and 7:2 begins with "make room for us." When the two phrases are placed together, they redundantly read "also open wide for us, make room for us." If a redactor were placing 2 Cor 6:14–7:1 in the midst of 2 Corinthians, it seems likely that this redundancy would be editorially removed, not added, whereas an author wishing to indicate a rhetorical *inclusio* would likely include this redundancy to ensure that the text conveyed where the "conscious stream" of the rhetoric ended and began again. In addition, as Cicero mentions in *De orator* 1.19, digressions are often used for the sake of comparison, which is precisely what 6:14–7:1 (specifically 6:14b–16a) does.

Several authors have argued that 6:14–7:1 is an interpolation and not a digression. Joseph A. Fitzmyer, "Qumran and the Interpolated Paragraph in 2 Corinthians 6:14–7:1," *Catholic Biblical Quarterly* 23, no. 3 (July 1961): 271–80, has proposed that 6:14–7:1 is a Qumran fragment, or at the least based on Qumranite literature. Fitzmyer's justification for this argument is based on certain congruencies between 2 Cor 6:14–7:1 and Qumranite literature: (1) there is a sharp dualism in both; (2) both oppose idolatry; and (3) both compare the people of their community to the temple of God. The first two reasons Fitzmyer presents exist throughout literature of the ancient world, and specifically Judaism in the Second Temple period; thus, they could virtually be applicable to any sect of Judaism in the Second Temple period. The third reason Fitzmyer presents is more convincing than the first two. However, he has neglected to mention that Paul may just be drawing upon a tradition similar to the Qumranite literature, not necessarily the corpus of Qumranite literature currently in our possession. Paul, throughout this passage, draws upon various traditions of his culture to explain his argument. Just because an author draws upon similar traditions to the Qumranites does not mean that there is an interpolation from Qumranite literature, or even that the author drew upon such literature as a source. To accept Fitzmyer's argument requires seriously limiting the scope of traditions in the *ethos* of the Second Temple period.

Hans Dieter Betz, "2 Cor 6:14–7:1: An Anti-Pauline Fragment?" *Journal of Biblical Literature* 92, no. 1 (March 1973): 88–108, also has argued that 6:14–7:1 is an interpolation. Betz claims that there is a major theological divergence in the passage from Paul's other writings; this divergence, he claims, is not only un-Pauline but also anti-Pauline. Betz presents the argument that 6:14–7:1 fits best with the arguments of Paul's detractors in Gal 2. Although there are some strong ties between the Galatian conflict at Antioch and the theology of 2 Cor 6:14–7:1, there is no explanation of how this anti-Pauline passage made its way into 2 Corinthians. Furthermore, if a redactor of 2 Corinthians was going to choose to insert such a passage, it seems likely that he would have indicated that he was doing so—or at least that it would be evident somewhere in vast New Testament manuscript tradition. Why would an editor insert something that opposes an author's viewpoint in the middle of the author's argument with no explanation or notation? It also seems far more likely that an anti-Pauline fragment would be inserted into Galatians than be inserted haphazardly into a letter directed at an entirely separate community, which may or may not have known of the Galatian conflict.

Even if an interpreter wishes to deny that 2 Cor 6:14–7:1 is a digression and affirm that it is an interpolation by an redactor, that interpreter still has to explain why the redactor chose to place this passage here.

9. The phrase "in the fear of God" could mean that "holiness" is "brought to completion" by means of one of three ways: (1) *by means of* "fear of God"; (2) in *the locative sphere of* "fear of God"; or (3) *because of* "fear of God." Most commentators seem to feel the need to choose between one of these syntactical options, and drastically overlook that the author may have intentionally been ambiguous in his language to show that all three options are at work. For an example, see Murray J. Harris, *The Second Epistle to the Corinthians: A Commentary on the Greek Text*, New International Greek Testament Commentary (Grand Rapids: Eerdmans, 2005), 513.

It is *by means of* and in *the locative sphere of* "fear of God" that "holiness" is "brought to completion," but it is also *because of* (or *out of*) "fear of God" that the Corinthian community should choose to cleanse themselves from "defilement." Although this ambiguity seems to be intentional, the author does give some clue as to which option is paramount in his thinking. The dualistic language of the author, which consequently results in a physical and theological separation between believers and unbelievers, suggests that the *locative sphere of* "fear of God" is the primary syntactical value being exercised.

10. *Aphorizō*, also as an aorist imperative, is used in Acts 13:2, in which Barnabas and Saul (Paul) are "set apart" for ministry. They're separated from others for the purpose of ministry. This usage is paralleled in Paul's own letters. In Galatians 1:15 Paul uses the verb (as a participle) to talk about being set apart for the gospel before he was born. In Romans 1:1 Paul uses the verb (again as a participle) to talk about being set apart for the

sake of the gospel. Also, in Galatians Paul uses the verb to talk about Peter separating from non-Jewish people after Jewish people arrive.

In Acts 19:9 the verb is used to talk about Paul separating from a group of people in the synagogue who are stubborn and continue in their unbelief, speaking evil of those who believe in Jesus.

In parallel to 2 Cor 6:14–7:1, Matt 25:32 uses the verb *aphorizō* to talk about the separation of the sheep from the goats. Here Jesus is talking about the final judgment and the separation of those who truly follow him and those who do not. The context, similar to the larger context in 2 Corinthians, is about those who embrace Jesus' ways (caring for the impoverished) and those who do not.

In Luke 6:22 Jesus uses the verb to speak about those who exclude his followers—so this is an exclusion that goes the opposite way (unbelievers removing themselves from believers).

11. The verb *heterozygeō* (ἑτεροζυγέω) is not found elsewhere in biblical Greek or Greek literature, as Harris notes; he then proceeds to list several different options for translating the term *heterozygountes* (ἑτεροζυγοῦντες). The example of Lev 19:19, used in this work, is an adjectival use of a word in the same semantic domain. I have used this particular example, because in agreement with Harris, I think that Paul is alluding to Lev 19:19 and Deut 22:10—showing that believers and unbelievers "result in an incongruous mismatch ... ill-matched union ... total dissonance," as Harris says. See Murray J. Harris, *The Second Epistle to the Corinthians: A Commentary on the Greek Text*, New International Greek Testament Commentary (Grand Rapids: Eerdmans, 2005), 498–99.

12. These are not the only options available, but they seem to be the most probable, since only these two can be fully substantiated on the basis of 2 Corinthians. This does not rule out the possibility that the Corinthian community applied this text to other kinds of unbelievers, or even that Paul understood that it could be applied to other kinds of unbelievers.

13. Paul's most lengthy discussion of the relationship between believers and unbelievers is in 1 Corinthians; naturally, 2 Corinthians picks up on this discussion. But Paul also discusses unbelievers elsewhere in his letters. In Titus, Paul makes a remark that directly parallels 2 Cor 6:14–7:1: "To the

pure all things are pure, but to those who are defiled and unbelieving nothing is pure, but both their mind and conscience are defiled" (Titus 1:15). In 1 Timothy Paul shows the sharp contrast that should exist between a believer's life and an unbeliever's life when he says: "But if someone does not provide for his own relatives, and especially the members of his household, he has denied the faith and is worse than an unbeliever" (1 Tim 5:8).

It's also possible that "unbelievers" in 2 Corinthians is a reference to the "false apostles," but it seems that the term has broader connotations based on the usage elsewhere in Paul's letters. Nowhere does Paul use the term in a way that would narrow its focus to simply "false apostles." The usage in 2 Cor 4:4 further rules out this narrowing, since it is applied broadly there.

14. Of course, there are exceptions to statements (for example, 1 Cor 7:12–15) about staying married, such as when someone is abused by his or her spouse. In that case, divorce would be permitted. Paul also clarifies that the unbelieving spouse is the one who consents to staying married, noting: "But if the unbeliever leaves, let him leave. The brother or the sister [in Christ] is not bound in such cases" (1 Cor 7:15).

15. This is a small (not even close to comprehensive) list of the temples, altars, and tributes present in Corinth ca. AD 50–100: a temple to Tychē, the Bath of Eurycles, the Peribolos of Apollo, the Fountain of Peirene, a Propylaea, a statue of Athena, an unidentified altar, a Babbius monument, a Fountain of Poseidon (Neptune), a temple of the imperial cult, an Aphrodite temple, and a Sarapis shrine. This evidence is abstracted from J. Murphy O'Connor, "Corinth," *ABD* 1:1134–39.

16. It's possible that the "super-apostles" ("preeminent apostles") and the "false apostles" are actually two different groups. However, the parallel usage of the terms makes this unlikely. Either way, it's clear that Paul has adversaries at Corinth who seem to be undermining his authority. The exact identity of these "super-apostles" or "false apostles" is unknown. For the various interpretation options, and the major commentators that argue for each one, see Derek R. Brown, Wendy Widder, and E. Tod Twist, *Lexham Bible Guide: 2 Corinthians*, ed. John D. Barry and Douglas Mangum (Bellingham, WA: Lexham Press, 2013).

17. My own translation.

18. The polemic viewpoint of light versus darkness is common in literature of the period (e.g., John 1:5; 1QS 3.13–26; 1QM).

19. In the OT, the term Belial is used, not Beliar, but the two terms seem too close in sound to not see some sort of connection. In Deuteronomy 13:13 Belial refers to "worthless" or "lawless" men. Belial is also an evil figure in wider Judaism at the time of Paul. Also, the book of *Jubilees* depicts Beliar as an actual figure, speaking of a "spirit of Beliar" (*Jubilees* 1:20), although it is possible that "spirit" here might simply be an aesthetic way of indicating certain kinds of action. As my colleague Derek R. Brown reminded me, Annette Steudel convincingly argues that "Belial" is the most frequently used name for the chief malevolent figure within the Qumran literature (Annette Steudel, "God and Belial," *The Dead Sea Scrolls Fifty Years after their Discovery: Proceedings of the Jerusalem Congress, July 20–25, 1997*, ed. Lawrence H. Schiffman, et al. [Jerusalem: Israel Museum, 2000], 332–40). Passages in view here, as Brown also pointed out to me, include: 1QS 1:16–18; 3:13–4:26; CD 2:19; 4:12–19; 5:18; 12:2–3; 1QM 1:1–5; 13:4, 10–12; 18:1–3. This connection means that Paul very well could have viewed Belial (or Beliar as he calls the figure) and Satan as synonymous. Either way, it's clear that Beliar and Satan are part of the same sphere in 2 Corinthians because they represent the same kind of negative actions; both are opposed to Christ's work. See Derek R. Brown, *"The God of This Age": Satan in the Churches and Letters of the Apostle Paul*, Wissenschaftliche Untersuchungen zum Neuen Testament II (Tübingen: Mohr Siebeck, forthcoming).

20. Interestingly, like 2 Corinthians, the *Testament of Joseph* 20:2 equates the Lord with "light" and Beliar with "darkness." This suggests that Paul may be redacting an oral or written source of his time by substituting Christ for Lord. If this is the case, this shows just how powerful Paul thinks Christ truly is.

21. The closing phrase of 2 Cor 6:18 ("says [the] Lord Almighty") is most likely from 2 Sam 7:8, since the second half of 2 Cor 6:18 quotes 2 Sam 7:14.

Paul clarifies the grounds for his authority by introducing and concluding his scriptural citations with a statement that indicates that the Scriptures come by means of the Lord (6:16c; 6:18b) and by inserting the "messenger formula" in the middle of the verse to indicate that he is an agent of the Lord, who has the authority to appropriate these Scriptures in their new context (6:17b). By using the "messenger formula," he is demanding that they respect his authority on this matter, since it is an oracle from "[the] Lord" (6:17-18). The "messenger formula" occurs in this exact form 844 times in the Hebrew Scriptures; for examples, see Exod 4:2; Josh 7:13; 2 Sam 7:5; 1 Kgs 13:21; 1 Chr 11:4; Isa 52:3; Jer 2:5; Ezek 20:3; Hos 2:21. It is used to indicate that the words being spoken by an individual (usually a prophet) are directly from the Lord (i.e., they are a divine oracle).

22. Paul declares—through evoking the covenant formula— that God will be among his people and possess them; likewise, his people will possess him (6:16; 6:18).

This covenant formula tradition was widespread at the time 2 Corinthians was being written. In *Baruch* 2:35, for example, God says, "I will be their God and they shall be my people; and I will never again remove my people Israel from the land that I have given them" (*Baruch* 2:35); 1Q22 f1ii:1 says, "[I]srael and hear! This very [da]y [you become a peo]ple belonging to the Lord [your God], so [you] should o[bserve my regulations] and my testimonies [and] my [commandments]" (Michael Wise, Martin Abegg, Jr., and Edward Cook, *The Dead Sea Scrolls: A New Translation* [New York: HarperCollins, 2005], 207). Second Corinthians 6:16d is a conflation of Lev 26:11-12 and Ezek 37:27. An examination of Ezek 37:27 reveals that the writer may be engaging in intertextual dialogue with Lev 26:11-12; if this is the case, Paul is merely continuing this tradition of intertextual dialogue. Paul's interpretive method of Scripture, where he uses it primarily to make his own case, is also very common in the period: See John D. Barry, "Early Evidence of Subjective Interpretation in the Subjective Interpretation in the Pesharim of Qumran," *Revue Scriptura*, new series 9 (2007): 119-38.

The "covenant formula" is indicated by the possessive genitives in 6:16 (e.g., "their God" and "my people") and the datives of possession in 6:18 (e.g., "to you a father" and "to me sons and daughters"). This is all depicted as coming by means of God's ability to "transcend" into the world and "dwell among" his people (6:16). The covenant tradition is appropriated to reveal the way in which God "dwells" among the Corinthian *ecclesia* and all believers. This corresponds directly to the idea that the Corinthian community (including Paul) is a "temple of [the] living God" (6:16). Just as God dwelled in his temple in Jerusalem (1 Kgs 8:13), he now dwells in the Corinthian community.

Interestingly, 2 Corinthians 6:18 is primarily from 2 Sam 7:14 (also including an insertion from Isa 43:6), which is in the context of God making his covenant with David, concerning the temple and David's heir, Solomon. Also, in 6:17 Paul has reversed the order of Isa 52:11.

23. With his statement regarding God dwelling among his people, the author infers that it is imperative that God's people be "separate" from unbelievers (6:17). This verse is critical to understanding 2 Cor 6:14–7:1, since it involves a very important redaction by the author. The author has changed the verse from "come out from the middle of her" in the MT and the LXX, which is Babylon in the context of Isa 52:11, to "come out from the middle of them."

This is a drastic and daring change on behalf of Paul, which is perhaps why he chooses to insert the "messenger formula" here (2 Cor 6:17). Paul uses exilic language, directed against Babylon, and directs it at unbelievers. In doing so, he is essentially saying that associating oneself with unbelievers is equivalent to resorting back to a state of exile. Paul has radically recontextualized this passage in its new historical context. Paul reveals what will ultimately occur if the believers do not separate themselves from unbelievers; they will be spiritually exiled, by choice.

24. Paul infers that his Scripture citations in 6:16–18 are promises (7:1). These promises require action from the Corinthian believers. Paul uses these particular Scripture citations to bring up God's covenant with Israel—to further set up the need for the Corinthian believers to repent.

The covenant is acknowledged through the conflation of Ezek 37:27 and Lev 26:11–12 in 2 Cor 6:16. The redaction of Isa 52:11 in 2 Cor 6:17 reveals the form of repentance that needs to take place in the Corinthian community. It is then exposed, through the usage of Ezek 20:34, that this repentance will require very specific actions in 2 Cor 6:17. Then, in 6:18, through a redaction of 2 Sam 7:14 and Isa 43:6, God affirms his people, while expecting that they do what he has requested.

25. Ike Ndolo, "Offering," *Rivers* (Nashville: Ike Ndolo, 2013).

Paul's view of cleansing ourselves is clear based on the scriptural promises he cites and the action required to bring "holiness" to "completion." Holiness, in the levitical tradition— and as evoked in the scriptural elucidations—has to do with a separation from things that are "unclean" (e.g., Lev 11:44–45). Since this is the case, it is not surprising that Paul speaks about "holiness" being brought "to completion" through cleansing oneself of defilement.

## Chapter 3. A God Who Comforts Us in All Affliction

1. We know from Acts how difficult things were for Paul in the province of Asia. There was even a riot in Ephesus over the preaching of Paul and his colleagues (Acts 19:21–40). And from Paul's remarks in 2 Corinthians, there appear to have been even more difficulties in Asia (2 Cor 1:8).

The events Paul describes in 2 Corinthians likely all occur during his third missionary journey (ca. AD 52–57); Paul founded the church at Corinth during his second missionary journey (Acts 18; ca. AD 49–51). The likely sequence of events of Paul's third missionary journey, as involving the Corinthians, is as follows. Prior to his third missionary journey, Paul had a sorrowful visit with the Corinthians; we're not certain when this occurred (2 Cor 2:1). But despite his sorrowful visit, Paul had intended to go to Corinth right away during his third missionary journey, prior to visiting Macedonia (2 Cor 1:16). He may have intended to depart from the lower part of the province of Asia (modern-day Turkey), across the Aegean Sea—possibly from Ephesus. But Paul doesn't depart from Ephesus; instead he goes north to Troas.

It is at Troas that a door was opened for Paul "by the Lord"— and this may be how his plans changed (2 Cor 2:11). (It could be that Paul always planned to leave from Troas on his way to Corinth.) We also know that during his *second* missionary journey, while at Troas, Paul had a vision that led him to conclude that he should preach the gospel in Macedonia—so that parallel past event also could be coming into play in 2 Corinthians (Acts 16:18–10). Whatever happened at Troas, it's clear that Paul doesn't find Titus there, so he goes on across the Aegean Sea to Macedonia (modern-day northern Greece) instead of heading to Corinth. The mention of him not finding Titus at Troas is an important detail. Since Titus was at Corinth, and Paul did not find him at Troas, it could be that Paul's desire to know the state of things at Corinth (prior to his visit)—along with the divine direction he received—led to him changing his plans (2 Cor 7:13). (If this is the case, then it may be that Paul never intended to depart from somewhere like Ephesus to Corinth, but instead to go to Troas, meet Titus there, and then go with him to Corinth if all was well.)

Despite the lack of details about the various factors that led to Paul's change of plans, we know that he took the long way to Corinth: Rather than traveling by sea from the province of Asia to Achaia, Paul makes his way through Macedonia by land, south toward the province of Achaia, where Corinth is located. (Timothy and Silvanus are with Paul on this journey [2 Cor 1:19].)

Sometime after Paul lands in Macedonia, but before he has gone to Achaia, he writes 2 Corinthians. And it's sometime prior to going to Macedonia that Paul writes his "sorrowful letter." In line with the hypothesis that hearing from Titus was important to Paul (prior to going to Corinth) is the fact that he doesn't seem to know the Corinthians' response to his "sorrowful letter" when he decides to go straight to Macedonia. Titus seems to be the one who shares their response with him while he is in Macedonia (2 Cor 7:12–13).

Whatever Paul's exact planned route and the exact sequence of events, it's clear that the Corinthians knew his itinerary but that his plans later changed—leading them to question his motives and reliability. But Paul is equally clear that this change was divinely appointed (2 Cor 2:12, 14). It was not his choosing, but God's.

The exact chronology of events surrounding Paul's missionary journeys are very complicated and have resulted in much debate. For an overview of this debate, see Derek R. Brown, Wendy Widder, and E. Tod Twist, *Lexham Bible Guide: 2 Corinthians*, ed. John D. Barry and Douglas Mangum (Bellingham, WA: Lexham Press, 2013).

2. Paul uses "we" throughout 2 Corinthians because it's actually a coauthored work with Timothy. Throughout the majority of Paul's ministry, he mentored Timothy. Paul believed so much in Timothy that he left him to appoint leaders at the church at Ephesus (1 Tim 1:3).

> Timothy was the son of a Jewish mother and a Greek father. He lived in the city of Lystra, which is where he met Paul. Both Timothy's mother and grandmother were believers in Jesus (2 Tim 1:5). Timothy wasn't brought up as a law-abiding Jew and wasn't circumcised, which made his ministry among Jewish people

difficult (Acts 16:3; 2 Tim 3:15). Paul looks to
Timothy to finish the work they had begun in
Ephesus, telling Timothy to do the work of an
evangelist (2 Tim 4:5; John D. Barry et al., eds.,"1
Timothy—A Call to Sound Teaching," *DIY Bible
Study* [Bellingham, WA: Lexham Press, 2014]).

Since Paul appears to be the primary author of
2 Corinthians, he will be the focus of this book, not Timothy.
However, it's safe to say that most of what is said about Paul,
based on the context of 2 Corinthians, could also be applied
to Timothy. The viewpoint in 2 Corinthians likely would have
been representative of both of their viewpoints, feelings, and
opinions. However, Paul also seems to make a distinction between himself and Timothy, sometimes using "I" instead of
"we." For example, in 1 Cor 1:13, Paul briefly moves from "we"—
which he used in 1 Cor 1:3–9—to "I." He regularly makes the
same switch throughout his letters (see especially in 2 Cor 2:1–
11, where it's clear only Paul is speaking; compare 2 Cor 2:17).
It appears that whenever 2 Corinthians uses the first-person
singular ("I"), it's Paul speaking, and each time the letter uses
the first-person plural ("we"), it's referring to both Paul and
Timothy—unless it's clearly a reference to all Christians (or at
least himself, Timothy, and the believers he is addressing). Paul
also makes several inclusive statements referring to all believers (see 2 Cor 7:1).

3. My own translation.

4. Trent Reznor (Nine Inch Nails), "Hurt," *The Downward Spiral*
(Santa Monica, CA: Interscope Records, 1995). A repenting but
still troubled Johnny Cash famously covered this song near
the end of his life; the lyrics quoted here are actually the version Cash sang (he slightly changed Reznor's version; Johnny
Cash, *American IV: The Man Comes Around* [Santa Monica, CA:
American Recordings, Universal Music Group, 2002]).

5. "The Downward Spiral" is actually the title of the Nine
Inch Nails album that includes the song "Hurt." I highly rec-
ommend that depressed people not listen to depressing music. Christians need to be careful about what lyrics they allow
into their minds. Some songs can be detrimental to a believer's
demeanor and outlook, and some might even be a vehicle for
inviting in more demons. Music certainly was a vehicle for indulging my demons during my time of depression.

6. See Craig G. Bartholomew, *When You Want to Yell at God: The Book of Job* (Bellingham, WA: Lexham Press, 2014). As I was personally working through Job, I was using Charles R. Swindoll, *Job: A Man of Heroic Endurance* (Nashville: Thomas Nelson, 2004).

7. In retrospect, it's easy to see how good my traumatizing breakup was for me. Without the breakup, my relationship with Jesus would have likely been forever stilted: My relationship with my high school girlfriend was keeping me from living fully for Jesus (2 Cor 6:14). In addition, without the breakup, I would have never met my future wife, Kalene, whom I cannot imagine life without. Kalene and I were clearly meant for one another—being with her has brought me closer to Jesus and taught me how to truly love. Kalene leads me closer to Jesus, calling me to live more in God's image.

8. Mumford and Sons, "Awake My Soul," *Sigh No More* (London: Eastcote Studios, 2009).

## Chapter 4. Defending Ourselves like Paul Would

1. Tony Cummins (who publishes under Anthony Cummins) is the professor who made this remark, sometime in spring semester 2006 in his New Testament theology course.

2. "While Paul may be referring to 1 Corinthians here, he is probably referring to another letter written between 1 and 2 Corinthians. It is also possible that he is referring specifically to [2 Corinthians] 10–13, a section that corresponds to Paul's 'distressed' and 'anguished' description (v. 4)" (John D. Barry, ed., *Faithlife Study Bible* [Bellingham, WA: Lexham Press, 2012], 1 Cor 2:3).

3. Corinthians 2:5–11 is addressed in chapter 5, "Zebras, Lions, and Theology."

4. Route has been significantly simplified for ease of reading.

5. Route has been significantly simplified for ease of reading.

6. Rend Collective Experiment, "The Cost," *Homemade Worship by Handmade People* (Colorado Springs, CO: Kingsway Music, 2012)

7. This is an echo of the sentiment of Rend Collective Experiment's song "The Cost" (see previous note). Jesus makes this principle clear in Luke 9:57–62.

8. There were both Jewish and non-Jewish believers in the Corinthian church. Paul's ministry at Corinth first focused on the Jewish population (Acts 18:5).

9. For more on Paul's view of the law, see appendix A, "Flesh and Law in Paul's Theology."

10. Later on, Paul notes that these leaders are spreading a false gospel (2 Cor 11:4-7). See my discussion on this in chapter 10, "Super-Apostles and Boasting in Jesus."

## Chapter 5. Zebras, Lions, and Theology

1. Even if the man "cast to Satan" from 1 Cor 5:1-13 is not the same person Paul is talking about in 2 Cor 2:5-11, it's still an interesting parallel passage. When we examine the two passages together, we get a view of Paul rejecting someone and Paul accepting someone who has previously been rejected. Even if they're different people, we still see Paul's holistic perspective on reconciliation while maintaining the sanctity of the church.

There are other suggestions for the identity of the offender mentioned in 2 Cor 2:5-11. These interpretive options include, but are not limited to a man connected with the sexual misconduct going on at Corinth; someone advocating for visiting Corinthian temples (and participating in the sexual activities there); one of Paul's adversaries from his "sorrowful visit" (or shortly thereafter); someone who misappropriated funds from the Jerusalem offering; and even someone who is not part of the congregation at all.

2. Paul elsewhere talks about how he is "the foremost" of sinners—a reference to his life persecuting the Church prior to coming to Christ (1 Tim 1:15). In the same passage, he details how wonderful the grace of God is (1 Tim 1:12-17). In light of this, it seems unlikely that Paul would exclude someone from the Christian community merely for sinning. Thus, the man Paul tells the Corinthians to exclude from their community is likely openly, and repeatedly, sinning (1 Cor 5:1-5). It's also possible that the man has committed a sin so horrendous that the community must disassociate from him in order to preserve their reputation or for safety. Although this might be part of why Paul tells them to disassociate from the man, it seems that the larger purpose is "so that his spirit may be saved in the day of the Lord"—i.e., exclusion from the Christian community

is meant to make him recognize his sin and return to Jesus (1 Cor 5:5).

In talking about casting the man to Satan, Paul could mean one of several things: "[Paul may be suggesting that the community allow for] the sinful man to be prosecuted by Satan; if this is the case, then Paul is using the term in the same way as the book of Job (1:6–2:8). Paul may also be suggesting that those outside the community of believers belong to the realm of Satan (see 2 Cor 6:14 and 1 Tim 1:20). In that scenario, Paul would be suggesting that the sinner be handed over to the realm of sin ruled by the evil one (Satan). It's also possible that both ideas are at work. … Paul [also] could be indicating that when people are part of the believing community, they cannot be prosecuted by Satan; when [people] aren't [part of the believing community], [Satan] is free to do as he wishes. Thus, when the sinful man is handed over to the realm of evil and realizes how terrible it is to be prosecuted and subsequently judged, he will then choose to repent and return" (John D. Barry, ed., *Faithlife Study Bible* [Bellingham, WA: Lexham Press, 2012, 1 Cor 5:5]).

3. *The Lord of the Rings: The Two Towers*, directed by Peter Jackson (Los Angeles: New Line Cinema, 2002).

4. Beryl Markham, *West with the Night* (Boston: Houghton Mifflin, 1942; repr., New York: Farrar, Straus & Giroux, 2013).

5. Of course, there are extreme cases that churches must address, like those involving previous sex offenders or those who have committed violent crimes. Every church should make safety a major priority, especially the safety of their children and any others who are vulnerable in their community. Churches should have safety protocols in place and require background checks for leaders and staff (and contractors who are on site).

## Chapter 6. Who Do You Work for—Really?

1. This idea is influenced by the February Birds' song "Christ in the Middle" (*Souls & Streets Where Hope Moves*, Bellingham, WA: February Birds, 2013).

2. See Michael Heiser, "Who is the God of this World?," *Bible Study Magazine*, January/February 2014, 44–45. Although some of the church fathers believed that God was the god of this

world mentioned in 2 Cor 4:3–4, Heiser argues that Paul is referring to Satan—an argument I agree with:

> The context of Ephesians 2:1–2 is similar to that of 2 Corinthians 3–4: It explains why people do not believe the gospel and even oppose it. Since Paul's use of *theos* in Philippians 3:19 shows us the term could be used to speak of controlling a dominion, Satan could easily be described with that term because he rules over unbelievers (Heiser, "Who is the God of this World?," 45).

3. I am sure that I am not the first to make this point, but I cannot recall where I first encountered this idea. John Bunyan, *Pilgrim's Progress* (1678; repr., London: James Clarke, 1987) illustrates this point well. Likewise, there is a parallel in *The Two Towers* (directed by Peter Jackson; Los Angeles: New Line Cinema, 2002) when Samwise Gamgee talks about the characters in the stories of old who experienced great trials.

4. For more on Paul's use of the term "flesh," see the appendix, "Flesh and Law in Paul's Theology."

5. My own translation.

6. My own translation.

## Chapter 7. Joy, Grief, and Making Peace

1. See John 1:4–5; compare John 12:46 and 1 John 1:5–8.

2. "Titus accompanied Paul to Jerusalem where the apostles Peter, James, and John affirmed Paul's ministry to the Gentiles (Gal 2:1–10). Titus also served as Paul's representative to the church in Corinth, where he collected relief funds for the poor church in Jerusalem (2 Cor 8:6–7). Because of his character and dedication, the apostle and the churches held Titus in high regard (2 Cor 8:18–19)" (ed. John D. Barry, "Titus," *Faithlife Study Bible* [Bellingham, WA: Lexham Press, 2012], Titus 1:4).

3. Paul Williams and Kenneth Ascher, "Rainbow Connection," *The Muppet Movie* (Los Angeles, CA: Henderson Associates; London: ITC Entertainment, 1979).

4. From the *Faithlife Study Bible*: "The Hebrew word translated *qasht* is most frequently used of an archer's bow. The appearance of "cloud" clearly indicates a rainbow, but the military connotation may still be present. The rainbow may symbolically speak of God's war bow—God's wrath has ended and He

has hung up His bow" (ed. John D. Barry; *Faithlife Study Bible* [Bellingham, WA: Lexham Press, 2012], Gen 9:13).

5. Both Jude and Peter (Jude 1:5; 1 Pet 3:18–20; 2 Pet 2:4–5) use the Noah motif to explain this exact concept, so from a biblical theology perspective it's reasonable to think that Paul's ideas about separation from evil (and corrupt teachers) would align with similar ideas. Paul himself does not use the language of the flood—so the language here is evoked by way of analogy and to make some biblical theology connections that seem probable (see John D. Barry and Miles Custis, *2 Peter & Jude: Contend for the Faith*, Not Your Average Bible Study Series [Bellingham, WA: Lexham Press, 2014]).

## Chapter 8. How to Love the Impoverished

1. The churches in Macedonia include the church in Philippi, Thessalonica, and Berea (Acts 16:11–17:15; 20:1–6). Paul visited these churches on his second and third missionary journeys. In this instance, he is referring to his second trip.

2. Chart from John D. Barry, ed., *Faithlife Study Bible* (Bellingham, WA: Lexham Press, 2012), 1 Cor 2:13.

3. See Steve Corbett and Dr. Brian Fikkert, *When Helping Hurts* (Chicago: Moody, 2009), and Robert Lupton, *Toxic Charity* (San Francisco: HarperCollins, 2012).

4. Eugene Cho of One Day's Wages often says similar things on his blog and on Facebook. I was saying these same kinds of remarks prior to reading his thoughts, but hearing it from him makes me think that the toxic spirit of so-called "critique" is something that leaders everywhere deal with.

5. *Faithlife Study Bible* provides a good summary of the interpretive options for this famous brother: "The identity of this "brother" in Christ is unknown. He may have been Apollos (Acts 18:24–28), Timothy (a co-sender of 2 Corinthians; 1:1), or one of Paul's Macedonian traveling companions listed in Acts 19:29. The fact that Paul does not mention his name probably indicates that the church already knew him" (ed. John D. Barry, *Faithlife Study Bible* [Bellingham, WA: Lexham Press, 2012], 2 Cor 8:18).

6. Paul refers to the three men as "messengers of the churches," or, more literally "apostles of the churches." This could mean that they're apostles (in the sense of the church office) or

that they're "sent ones" from the churches—hence the English translation "messengers." With the famous speaker included, as well as Titus, the term "apostle" in the sense of a "church office" seems like the more probable interpretation.

7. Abraham Kuyper, "Sphere Sovereignty," *Abraham Kuyper: A Centennial Reader* (ed. James D. Bratt; Grand Rapids: Eerdmans, 1998), 461–90. This quote echoes, "The earth is Yahweh's, with its fullness, *the* world and those who live in it" (Psa 24:1; compare Pss 50:12; 89:11).

## Chapter 9. Fighting the Spiritual War against Darkness

1. For more on Paul's use of the term "flesh," see the appendix, "Flesh and Law in Paul's Theology."

2. My own translation, or better put, slight paraphrase based on the immediate context and ideas.

3. John D. Barry et al., eds., "2 Corinthians—A Call to Reconciliation," *DIY Bible Study* (Bellingham, WA: Lexham Press, 2014).

4. See "Satan and the Messiness at Corinth" in chapter 5, "Zebras, Lions, and Theology."

## Chapter 10. Super-Apostles and Boasting in Jesus

1. I lean toward the interpretation that Paul is speaking of someone else, since prior to this he has been speaking in the first person. In addition, his statement in 2 Cor 11:5 seems to favor this view: He would boast about this person's spiritual experience, but not about his own. In addition, Paul emphasizes that he does not wish for anyone to think more of him than what they see and hear—what they can attest to through experience (2 Cor 11:6). Nonetheless, it's certainly possible that the event is so "spiritual" in nature that Paul wishes to distance himself in the telling of it, so that the Corinthians don't obsess over this story. For more on what Paul means by "third heaven" and how to interpret this event, see Appendix B: Miles Custis and John D. Barry, "Paul and the 'Third Heaven,'" *Faithlife Study Bible*, ed. John D. Barry (Bellingham, WA: Lexham Press, 2012).

2. This is essentially the same point that Paul's statements in 2 Cor 6:14–7:1 emphasize. Christ is the thing to be most valued

and is the only thing we should center ourselves on. Strength from anywhere else is merely Satan deceiving us.

3. Faithlife Study Bible summarizes the possible interpretations: "This 'thorn' may refer to Paul's inner emotional turmoil about the churches (2:4), ... his opponents (like the false apostles; 11:1–5), a physical ailment (such as poor eyesight), his speaking ability (10:10), or demonic opposition (both in general or specific to him, as in 1 Thess 2:18). ... The word ... 'messenger' [may refer to] a demonic entity ... troubling Paul. It's also possible that this language may simply be metaphorical, referring to the affliction rather than a supernatural enemy. However, even the metaphorical language seems to necessitate some kind of real affliction, which itself could be a type of demonic manifestation in Paul's mind or spirit. He is praying for it to leave him. If Paul does have an evil being in mind, it could be tempting him, causing physical pain, or pointing out his past (and current) wrongdoings in a way that makes him feel guilty rather than free (making it difficult for him to fully experience the grace of Christ). ... By using the term 'Satan' [*Satanas*] Paul likely has in mind the evil being that is the antithesis of God's work in the world. It appears that this being sent another evil being (a demon) to antagonize Paul. Alternatively, Paul may be using the term *Satanas* here as simply 'prosecutor' or 'accuser,' not referring to an evil spiritual being. ... [But since] Paul elsewhere appears to use the term for the actual evil being (11:14; compare note on 1 Cor 5:5; also see 1 Cor 7:5; 2 Cor 2:11) ... [and since] Paul connects this being with the serpent that deceived Eve (see 11:3) ... [it seems more likely that he means Satan as an evil figure]" (John D. Barry, ed., Faithlife Study Bible [Bellingham, WA: Lexham Press, 2012], 2 Cor 12:7).

4. This point is well illustrated in Brennan Manning's work *Ruthless Trust* (Grand Rapids: Zondervan, 2009), which influenced my thought on this matter.

5. Adapted from John D. Barry, ed., *Faithlife Study Bible* (Bellingham, WA: Lexham Press, 2012), 2 Cor 12:7.

6. See Neil T. Anderson, *The Bondage Breaker* (Eugene, OR: Harvest House, 2006). This book explores in detail the ways that Christians are oppressed by evil and how they can be free from it. This is a helpful resource for anyone dealing with ongoing sin or felt oppression.

7. William Wilberforce, *A Practical View of Christianity* (1797; repr., Peabody, MA: Hendrickson, 1996), 32.

8. Paul further makes the point in this passage that Titus and the brother who came with him acted according to "the same spirit," taking the same steps Paul did—they too ministered freely (2 Cor 12:18).

9. Disorder seems like an oddity in Paul's list of sins in 12:20. But when we look back to 1 Corinthians and see the issues affiliated with disorderly worship, it's easy to understand what he means (see 1 Cor 11–14; compare Gal 5:19–20).

10. See "Overview" in chapter 1, "The Threads of Life."

## Chapter 11. Conclusion

1. *The Lord of the Rings: The Return of the King*, directed by Peter Jackson (Los Angeles: New Line Cinema, 2003).

## Appendix A. Flesh and Law in Paul's Theology

1. My own translation.

2. Steven E. Runge, "Spirit and Flesh in Paul's Letters," *Faithlife Study Bible,* ed. John D. Barry (Bellingham, WA: Lexham Press, 2012).

3. Derek R. Brown, *"The God of This Age": Satan in the Churches and Letters of the Apostle Paul,* Wissenschaftliche Untersuchungen zum Neuen Testament II (Tübingen: Mohr Siebeck, forthcoming). See chapter 5, "Zebras, Lions, and Theology."

4. There is much debate about Paul's view of the law in 2 Corinthians. This debate is summarized well in Derek R. Brown, Wendy Widder, and E. Tod Twist, *Lexham Bible Guide: 2 Corinthians,* ed. by John D. Barry and Douglas Mangum (Bellingham, WA: Lexham Press, 2013), which reads:

> Scholars as early as Origen (ca. AD 250) interpreted Paul's claim [in 2 Corinthians 3:6] to be … [a contract between] a 'literal' (the 'letter') approach to Scripture with a 'spiritual' or allegorical approach. …
>
> Most interpreters since the Reformation have understood Paul to be contrasting the old and the new covenants. Within this general agreement are at least three views on what Paul meant. The first perspective is that Paul

was contrasting the law (the 'letter') and the gospel (the 'Spirit'). ... The purpose of the law is to drive people to the gospel and its message of forgiveness and power. However, many scholars are uncomfortable with such a negative understanding of the law and do not believe it accurately represents the OT portrayal of the law or Paul's broader view of it. They contend that Paul did not mean the law itself, but rather a legalistic distortion of the law by post-exilic Judaism ... the problem with the 'letter' is that humans relied on themselves to keep it, not on the power of the Spirit.

A third interpretation is that Paul was describing two epochs of salvation history. In this view, his emphasis was not on the content of each covenant, but rather on their characteristics. The old covenant, inscribed on stone (2 Cor 3:3), was an external covenant, while the new covenant was inscribed on flesh (2 Cor 3:3). The weakness of the old covenant was not what it said; it was the nature of the people who tried to keep it.

Here, I essentially propose that Paul had all three interpretive options in mind.

5. Nijay K. Gupta, "The Torah: Like a Spare Tire," *Bible Study Magazine*, September/October 2010, 31.

## Appendix B. Paul and the "Third Heaven"

1. John D. Barry and Miles Custis, "Paul and the 'Third Heaven,'" in *Faithlife Study Bible* (ed. John D. Barry, Michael S. Heiser, Miles C. Custis, Douglas Mangum, Matthew M. Whitehead, and Michael R. Grigoni, Bellingham, WA: Lexham Press, 2012).